HEALING THE HOLES IN MY HEART

HEALING THE HOLES IN MY HEART
(Completing the Circle of Personal Empowerment)

by

Elaine M. Bready

Creative Resources

Art illustrations by Alyce J. Blue
Cover design by Steve Mowles and Dolores Hoffman

Creative Resources
Mona L. Jeter, Publisher
P.O. Box 2318, North Highlands, California 95660
Request for orders should be addressed to Post Office Box 2318, North Highlands, California 95660. (916) 344-7546.

Printed in the United States of America
First Edition

Library of Congress Catalog No.: 91-74104
ISBN: 1-880388-35-9

Dedication

5

To
Erica and Al
for allowing me
to be
free ...

Art illustrations
by
Alyce J. Blue

Contents

Acknowledgments

I would like to express my deepest appreciation for their help, support, guidance, and encouragement in creating this book to: Liang Ho for her commitment and work in the cross cultural field. She helped me begin the discovery of the missing pieces of my cultural identity; to my publisher, Mona L. Jeter and editors Lois E. Rice, Adrienne R. Mervin and everyone at Creative Resources for their feedback, suggestions, and most of all, for their love and undying faith in my work; to Tana Marie Richards, for her spiritual guidance and inspiration; to Dixie Robertson and Nancy Enzler of Griffin Printing for their expertise, guidance, and reassurance; and especially to Truth Walker for being home when I arrived. Each of these people, and many who are not specically mentioned, have contributed immeasurably to my vision and to this book. My thanks to each of you always.

But above all, my eternal gratitude for the ever present unconditional love of my Higher Power.

Foreword

The journey inward to self is the greatest personal challenge we can experience. To find inner peace and happiness, to understand your purpose here on this earth, can encompass a lifetime of trying to come through your fears and be free of the pain of the holes in your heart. For whatever reason you chose these holes (the personal lessons you chose to learn in this lifetime), know that you can move through the void, out of the hole, and into enlightenment.

This very special book reflects Elaine's journey in healing the holes in her heart and reveals a way for us to also find our own personal truth. Oftentimes, the path is so simple, we walk right past it. Change begins with recognizing and owning our fears. New levels of truth will always be revealed as growth occurs. As Elaine helped me to see my "truth," I hope that by her book she can also help you see your "truth." As this Journey has been mine, may it also be yours.

From the bottom of my heart, Elaine, thank you.

L. E. Rice

Dear Readers,

Being able to survive trauma as we experienced it is often not enough to ensure healthy personal or interpersonal relationships. Healthy relationships begin with healthy selves.

You need not have experienced a deeply troubled and traumatic childhood to have painful wounds. Since most of us come from dysfunctional family systems and learn to survive within a dysfunctional society, we experience the spiritual, emotional, and physical pain of the holes in our hearts.

I've spent many years working with a lot of people helping them to resolve a variety of issues which resulted in feelings of anger, fear, hurt, and shame. In working with each person, I became increasingly aware of the depth of pain each experienced. While I used every skill and tool I had been taught as well as any information I continued to learn, I realized that using these tools exclusively was not enough. So I turned my attention to the very people I tried to help for the guidance and source of information that would best serve them. In so doing, I learned much about what they needed and wanted for themselves. I learned also that what they needed and wanted was not unlike what I needed and wanted.

I discovered the tremendous strength within each of these people. It takes incredible strength to endure and to survive physical, emotional, and psychological injuries. Through my teaching and counseling, I discovered a common place of pain that each of us experience.

Suddenly, the world began to take on a different shape and life began to reveal a different meaning to me. Rather than to view them as "those people," I began to see them as reflections of all of us. Who among us has not, in some way, felt helpless, hopeless, oppressed, and victimized?

I did not touch their pain-filled hearts with my intellect. I touched them in the same way that they touched me - with the heart. From our hearts, we began to discover the many holes that existed within them. The holes came as a result of many experiences. Their existence changed much about the way we see ourselves, and consequently, the way we see and treat others.

In teaching others, I often use my own personal experience to clarify a theory or philosophy. It isn't that the stories are in any way the end-all, be-all answers to a thousand questions. Sometimes the stories simply help to make the theory or philosophy real and tangible. It isn't that I have any of the answers to any of the questions about life, pain, anger, or fear. I have only my perceptions. Sharing stories has simply been a way to illuminate another possibility, another reality.

This book was written with that same intention. It is my belief that the answers lie within us all. We need but choose to look at them. This story is about how I came to recognize the holes in my heart; how I came to understand their existence; and how I began to heal them. It is not unlike your own story of personal growth and quest for personal empowerment. I wanted to write it because I simply wanted to share what I had learned. It is how I teach. It is how I have helped others to help themselves.

This story has no one message. There may even be no message for some. For others, there may be many messages. It is all in how you choose to perceive it. How you choose, is neither right nor wrong. It simply is.

There are many who have encouraged, supported and even firmly "nudged" me to write this story. Their love, compassion, and firmness is deeply felt and appreciated. There are many, many others whose lives I have been blessed to touch who have inspired and motivated me to continue my journey. Their strength of will and courage, I will always strive to emulate. Yet, there are many others who may never know just what our time together has given me.

My special gratitude to my parents, for they gave me life in the beginning and brought me to the beginning of my yellow brick road. They gave me gifts of strength, courage, and boldness of spirit, as well as a loving, compassionate, and nurturing heart. These gifts came as a result of the ways I have chosen to receive them.

My eternal gratitude to the men, women and children in my life who by their own lives and our willingness to explore possibilities together helped me to arrive here at this place. Though there may have been pain, anger, and sorrow, there was also incredible love, joy, and happiness. No time or interaction was irrelevant or insignificant because the meaning I have derived from our relationships has allowed me to heal the holes in my heart. I will forever be free as a result.

For their love, compassion, encouragement, and patience in listening to my story over and over and over again -- thank you Moni, Lois, Sharon, Alyce, and Truth Walker. Truly, you have been a creative resource. But most of all, for their continued persistence, guidance, and energy, as well as radiant illumination, my deepest appreciation to Ethan, Daniel, and Eileen. Together, I believe we can make a difference.

So, dear reader, whatever inspiration, message or enjoyment you find within these pages is just what you choose to find. It is all relevant in whatever form you require. My pleasure is in sharing the story. My joy is in understanding that we are all able to be truly empowered and free. My hope is that we will all be able to heal the holes in our hearts.

Love and Peace,

Elaine. M. Bready

HEALING THE HOLES IN MY HEART
(Completing the Circle of Personal Empowerment)

Introduction

Sitting here at the dining room table, I glance around me at my new surroundings. I live in a large beautiful house, totally unemployed, in the formative stages of beginning a company with a dear friend as a roommate. Between us, we have four children to support and neither of us experiences the anxiety or the fear that accompanies newly separated women. Between us, we have thirty-six years of marriage with no regrets, resentment, or bitterness as we look behind us to the men we left; traveling the new paths we have chosen. Between us, we have endured years of self-sabotage, and the burdensome role of caretaker, strong, capable, over-responsible, and domineering women. Labels given us and accepted by us. There will always be those who will never understand. For the first time in our lives, we can say with soul conviction - it really has little significance to us and to what we will accomplish.

What is significant is that we are not unlike thousands of people who have arrived where they began. The getting there was both painful and joyful, but not difficult. The difficulty was in the time-consuming search for home. The solution was in the acknowledgment that the search found us running far away from home. When we stopped running, we found all of the answers to the questions that started us running in the first place.

The wonderful thing about self-exploration and self-awareness is the treasure found in the understanding of lessons learned and the greater depth of compassion, love, and acceptance I found for myself. I visualize my life as one large college campus. Every event, every relationship, every emotion has been a course selected by me; some general education credits, others prerequisites to electives. As in my own college years, there were times I felt the need to change majors frequently as I continually pondered the questions, "What do you want to be when you grow up?" I was never able to adequately answer that question with any real self-satisfaction. So, I came up with all types of socially acceptable ideas and roles, none of which truly answered my own question.

The only answer which held the deepest conviction of self-truth was that I wanted to be "free to be." Until now, I had been unable to visualize a "productive" life where I was "free to be." Until now, I had not realized the cage I placed myself in; allowing my search for truth to lead me to believe external messages from both tangible and intangible sources. Until now, I had defined myself and my purpose by all the shoulds: of being female; of being a minority; or of being someone's child, wife, or mother.

Until now, I was unaware just how much I believed and lived these external messages. That is the way of self-discovery. Layer upon layer is peeled away and what remains is the essence of the self. The humor is in the awareness that while I protested and rebelled at the obvious, more uncomfortable roles, another par t of me continued the same traditional path very well disguised as the non-traditional woman.

It is little wonder that the personal search for truth appears difficult and awesome. The journey seems burdened with obstacles and barriers. The road appears never-ending and dangerous. The only difficulty is in where we look for the answers. The fear is in the unknown which always exists outside ourselves. The truth is that no one will ever love you more than you love yourself. The lessons I have learned bring me into closer alignment with the truth. It is because of the discovery of my inner self that I have arrived home where I began. It is because of my self-acceptance that I am able to let go of my chokehold on messages, roles, and relationships that no longer serve a purpose in my life. I am healing those wounds, those holes in my heart. I am free to be and more; I am whole, healthy and in harmony with myself.

ONE

DISCOVERING THE HOLES IN MY HEART

Chapter 1

Often, I have reflected just how the holes appeared in my heart. My life events did not seem traumatic by comparison to the events of many people I have counseled over the past decade. Of course, I realize now that trauma is as it is perceived, and that surviving trauma is not the return to self. Healing the wounds caused by the trauma is the return to self and the coming home.

When I was three, I ran away from home and I have been running ever since. I have always been running toward the illusionary pot of gold at the end of many rainbow; always running further away from myself in search of the me I believed lay waiting within that pot.

At age three, I began my solitary journey into a world of not belonging, where color, sex, and religion absolutely determined the height and breadth of one's dreams and reinforced the impenetrable barriers to ensure personal limitations. At age three, I began to realize that comfort and security were privileges, not rights. I began to realize that I was alone; not because I was abandoned by my parents, not because they withheld their love and concern; and not because they created any hardship. But because of some "insignificant mistake" made by a porter at a train station when he directed my father, who stood impeccable in his army uniform, to board the railroad car for non-whites and cargo. Because this man, my hero, who stood in the sun's rays filled with pride and respect for himself and his country was subjected to this "mistake." Because this country, which my father unquestionably defended, oppressed and limited his freedom to be. Because as I looked at the color of my skin, I saw the instant barriers being raised and I became angry.

I was angry at the porter, whose mistake was a reflection of our country's statement regarding people of color. I was angry at my father, for being colored because it meant that my hero was mortal and vulnerable and unable to prevent being subjected to these undeserved "mistakes." I was angry at myself, too; because I knew that even though I was brown, I was also yellow and looked like neither my mother nor father. I was angry because I could not see myself in either of my parents. I was neither African-American and Native-American like my father; nor was I Japanese like my mother. There was no label for me. If color was going to make such a difference, what color was I? It is a solitary journey a multi-cultural person walks. One filled with incredible self-loathing, sorrow, and loneliness.

The holes appeared leaving wounds that gaped. I ran away from the pain of not belonging in a world whose distorted labelling included black and white, exclusively. I ran away in search of understanding, acceptance, and identity. I ran away to find others like me ... a mirror reflection with some definition of what I might be. I ran away from a heritage I knew nothing about. I decided that it was not significant. I would not allow this small thing to cause me this pain. But what I could not run away from was the need to belong, to begin, to be. And through my denial of myself, my pain grew ... secretly and quietly laying dormant in the depths of my heart.

*****   *****   *****   *****   *****

At four, I ran away again, this time from my hospital crib. The stark white curtains billowed menacingly against the window in contrast to the blackness of the night. I was trembling. I was afraid and alone. They thought I was shivering from the fever. I was chilled by the terrifying aloneness of being four, alone, and sick. They came in fours, dressed in white, these giants looming dangerously close to me. They held me. They restrained me. I cried. I screamed. I felt the intensity of the weapon they carried. The sharp tip of the needle penetrated my skin. In fear and pain ... alone in my silence, I sobbed. My mother was alone, too, far away in another hospital bed. My sister and I had been left in the care of my aunt who could not allow the childhood disease of the measles to ruin her beauty salon business. So, we were admitted into the hospital.

My father was on his way across country to get us. But laying there, alone, frightened, and in pain, I knew only that I felt the emptiness of being

I learned that crying and fear meant being alone. I ran away from tears; and I hid my fears in the depths of my soul ...

unattached, unworthy, and lost.

I ran away again that night - away from the darkness and sobs unanswered, from the pain of fear unsoothed, and away from the closeness and security that caring arms can provide. I would survive this, too. I learned that crying and fear meant being alone. I ran away from tears; and I hid my fears in the depths of my soul ... tucked neatly next to my color identity in the hole in my heart.

*****   *****   *****   *****   *****

Running was getting easier to do with every painful event.

"I cannot feel your touch. Please stop crying," I said quietly to myself.

"They'll come again."

I sat staring through the glass, my hand pressed firmly against the window separating me from my sister. She was crying, saddened from the return to the children's home where we lived; the two of us with other children without parents.   My mother, still far away across the city, lay in the hospital unable to hold me, to hug me, to kiss me, or to touch my heart. My father, strong and noble, lived far away in another city unable to prevent the coldness of strangers from piercing my soul. My father who fought the great wars, defending and protecting the rights of sons and daughters to be, was prevented by this same country from being here where I needed him. None of that mattered to me. All I knew was that the nuns would be back. Those messengers of God, mysteriously hiding in the blackness of their robes, void of human features, save the face. They had no hearts I thought. Their arrival meant only that we could not hold each other, to comfort one another in our "orphanage," unless the crying stopped.

"Please give her back her stuffed animal..."

That day in the coldness of that Catholic children's home, I ran away again. Away from the God that would allow us no compassion, that would take our parents away, that would leave me alone again ... no home, no sense of belonging. I ran away from the hopelessness and the helplessness as I stared motionless through the glass that separated me from love. I ran into the safety of my hole, the darkness and solitude became comfortable. No tears, no fears, no pain, no needs, and today, no God.

24

Chapter 2

Life does go on, and as I grew, I left behind only the fleeting picture memories of those three runaway days. I became my own warrior living through my physical body. I placed less value on feeling and more on doing. I was the invincible combat soldier emulating the heroes all around me as I acted on wartime strategies on that small army post playground. Void of color and sex, only the strong survive. I was determined to be the best troop I could be - just like my father. For many years, I thought I was a boy, playing ball and climbing trees. I learned the messages that crying and whimpering were for weaker ones - the sissies, the whiners, the girls. Besides, I tried crying. I remembered cries unanswered. Being one of the guys meant belonging; and I belonged. Yet, every now and then, someone would remind me that I was a girl and that girls were supposed to be with girls. Being a girl, forced me out of the "gang." I wasn't sure how much I had in common with other girls; but it didn't seem that I had a choice.

I did have a girlfriend once. I loved her and she loved me. She was not tough like me; but she was okay for a girl. I knew that she loved me because of the way she cared about what I thought and what I did. She even rubbed my tummy once when I was nauseous during choir practice. She kept rubbing it until I felt better, even though the nuns told her to stop. She really loved me. I loved her enough to try a lot of new things. I even rode a horse once and I remember her laughter as I clumsily climbed onto this giant beast, trying unsuccessfully to hide my fear. She laughed with so much love that I laughed too; and before I could stop, I had been riding for hours. That is how our days were spent; laughing and experiencing everything in our two very different worlds. It was my first experience of being cared about for being me and not for what I could do.

And then the laughter stopped. She was gone. Not physically gone - just away from me. I stood that day, tears stinging my eyes and emptiness filling my heart as she explained she would not be allowed to be my friend because her father outranked mine. I thought again that there must be something terribly wrong with me. As she turned and walked away, I ran away ... fast, and hard, and breathlessly. I left behind my soul-filled laughter, my love for another female, and my trust in my openness. I ran once more into my hole and brought with me the battle-scarred wounds of love redefined, of self-unfulfilled, unloved. No more laughter, no more female companionship. Just the shadow of myself.

*****   *****   *****   *****   *****

From the depths of the hole in my heart surged an unconquerable rage at the rapist and then myself. The violation complete, I lay in my solitude paralyzed by the absolute loss of control over my body. My warrior spirit found comfort in my physical body as I strengthened and nurtured it. I was physically tough. I dared to test my body and my body responded confidently with growing courage. There was no need for emotional vulnerability. Now I lay defeated; a wounded warrior with a body that could not prevent the rapist from the penetrating force of the sexual violation. I ran away that day ... away from a body I could not depend on ... from my sexuality, which I perceived was of itself, weaker. Now in my heart, my wounded physical body found companionship with the scarred and battle-worn emotional body. Together, they hid in the blackness of the void in my heart.

Listening to the emotional pain and trauma of many rape victims, I know the many places we run away to hide. Like them, I learned that being female meant being vulnerable. Like them, I learned to distrust my judgment and felt betrayed by so many who would not, and in many cases, could not understand that what happened to us was neither solicited nor deserved.

Many women run away from their sexuality by creating a masculine mask and devaluing their physical femininity. My masculine physical being was unable to protect me and so there was no comfort in that hiding place. Other women drape their bodies in unattractive garments or surround themselves with excess weight in efforts to ward off any future "would-be" rapists. But I knew that rape was not a crime of sex; but a crime of violence. No disguise would protect me from being female. Still others, ran away from life altogether, withdrawing from living - living only within the shadow of existence.

From the depths of yet another hole, I emerged once again -- my warrior spirit relentless in the battle cry of my inconquerable soul.

From the depths of yet another hole, I emerged once again -- my warrior spirit relentless in the battle cry of my inconquerable soul. For when I ran, I ran away from my emotional and physical pain into the deep recesses of my intellect. I may have been wounded in my heart and body, but I believed that my mind was my own and no one would be able to take away the strength and power of the mind.

Chapter 3

Then came "love."

He was strikingly handsome. Although I had no interest in pursuing any relationship, I was drawn to his magnetism, his charm, and more, his athletic prowess. Before I was consciously aware, I had "fallen" in love with the college athlete; and to further my own ego, he had fallen in love with me ... this desirable, sought-after college cassanova. What a prize we found in each other! I lost myself in that relationship, at least the shell of what remained outside of the hole in my heart. Six months later, the relationship began to die and with it my freedom diminished daily as I gave away control of my life.

Being in a relationship, I discovered, gave me a sense of belonging - a need I had been looking to fill since I ran away at three. Being us, gave me acceptance, gave me an ethnic identity denied me by the culture at large.

Alone, I was neither accepted by whites or blacks. The vision of Martin Luther King's dream was my own illusion. I found that this vision was only true from within the boundaries of specific groups of which because of my mixed blood, I could not qualify. The pain of having been discriminated against was my own. The vision of equality was blurred by the painful rejection of a race I had come to empathize with, a family of people suffering from the same torment of oppression. Their rejection was as painful, if not more so, than the oppression itself ... for I was never going to be black enough.

And because he was in my life, the acceptance came, begrudgingly, but still enough to matter. Enough to sacrifice self-respect and self-esteem as a being ... as a female being. I accepted the demands of what to wear, where to be, of

This angel retrieved my semi-conscious body from the enveloping waters and returned me to myself.

designated friends, of where to go, and when. I gave away intellectual dreams in pursuit of his happiness. I became consumed with pleasing him so as to not lose him. I ignored the betrayal of trust, of the many others he allowed into the relationship.

I ignored the stranglehold of my personal freedom. My spirit weakened until there was only a faint memory of what used to be me.

Two years later, I am high within the Rocky Mountains as close to the heavens as I dare to go. It is here that I find peace of mind and heart. But on this day, my love, my identity, my self were rejected again. As I walked toward the raging river, I felt the surge of despair breaking free from my heart.

There is no more room in my heart to hide. There is only the void. I am los t in that darkness, wandering aimlessly. I am consumed with the emptiness of being unattached, of being unwanted, of being unloved. I begin to feel unworthy and undeserving of hope. I listen to the spirit of the river, its current fast and furiously cleansing the obstacles lying in its path. I wished to be cleansed; to rid myself of such negative, painful obstacles. I wished to purge my heart. I wished to die.

Someone was watching me, some self-appointed guardian angel. This angel retrieved my semi-conscious body from the enveloping waters and returned me to myself. I find myself soaked and shivering as I sit by the warmth of a blazing fire. I am stunned at the overwhelming reality of the suicide attempt. Flooding through the dams of a mind that could not be touched, came the acknowledgment that I had run away - too far this time. As I sat confused and in shock, I was further devastated by my inability to answer a simple question.

"Can you tell me what 'you' want?" I cry because I do not know. I know what he wants. I know what they want. I know what is expected of me. I know what I should do and be. I know what I should feel and think. But, I do not know what I want. I cry because no one has ever asked.

I guess at being thankful, I guess at the message being sent, I create an answer to the question, "What do you want?"

"I just want to be free to be ... ."

I cannot explain further because I do not know what free is ... because I do not know who me is ... and because I do not know what being is.

There came also a redefinition of my own femininity.

Chapter 4

I spent the next two years in counseling - rebuilding and redefining my self-esteem. I discovered an inner spirit that was determined to find its way. The rejection of my cultural heritage was devastating. Through my therapy, I came to accept how readily I had defined who I was by my own ethnic background. I came to understand how great a value our culture placed on labels and categories and in my need to belong, I had accepted these labels as truth. I was beginning to understand my unique position in the middle of the color continuum.

There came forgiveness of being a mixed blood. Yet, there was little understanding of the power of being born into the center of all peoples. I was able, though, to let go of the self-loathing as I came to dream Martin's dream once again. His vision became my own quest for justice and equality.

During my counseling sessions, I became aware of other women whose sense of femininity had not been sacrificed in order to be successful. I began to resolve the "feminine means weak and vulnerable" myth. There came also a redefinition of my own femininity. I found the inspiration in being of service to others; and with great fervor, my thirst for knowledge became unquenchable. In sharing my own experiences with others, I not only helped myself, but I believed I was able to help others like me. I began to see my life events from a different perspective.

Every relationship became a classroom for knowledge. Every experience, a lesson to learn. Love, as I had defined it, the merging of two beings, became unnecessary and unwanted. Merging meant the loss of myself and having just regained that part of me, I was unwilling to give away my heart again. Yet, my need for companionship and friendship remained an ever-growing hole in my heart.

As I continued my journey, I was determined to grow comfortable with myself and my journey. I immersed myself in myself in an attempt to quiet the gnawing in my soul. I focused on what I must accomplish with my life. At 22, I was driven and obsessed to make a diference.

Chapter 5

He entered my life in the quiet unassuming way that became character-istic of his love ... softly and unsure of himself. I overwhelmed him with my intellect and boldness of spirit. His gentleness and sensitivity drew from my heart a compassion and need for companionship that I struggled to keep away from myself. He listened to me. He listened for hours and hours, accepting my thoughts and feelings for what they were ... my own, without judgment, without labelling.

I felt deeply that his path had been a solitary one, and like mine, the loneliness was a consuming, ever-growing hole in his heart. I had found a kindred spirit. His mind, razor-sharp, drew me to his spirit as together we questioned and explored all the possibilities of our existence.

Within a few short months, love grew between us. I was both enamored and confused by his insecurities. This tall, intelligent, sensitive academy graduate was certainly unlike his narcissistic comrades. Because of my need to help others, and because I cared so deeply for this remarkable man, and because we filled the needs of one another completely; I believed that together, we could heal the holes in our hearts.

So, we sealed the bond we created; and began our lives together ... determined that we could conquer the world.

We never did get to those holes though. Looking back, what we did do was complete the circle of loneliness. Loving and living as deeply as we would allow ourselves to love. Still, the secrets remained. It was the secrets ... unspoken, unconfronted ... that forced each of us away from ourselves. We

I believed that together, we could heal the holes in our hearts.

lived together; we loved together; and we created life together defining and redefining ourselves to meet the growing needs of our subconscious secret selves.

I am not sure just when it was that I lost myself in him. I know that at first, his need for me was intense and complete. I needed to be needed ... to me that meant belonging. His need became love; and I fully embraced that love as the only definition of such a powerful emotion.

Because he was not overtly demanding, I never saw his love as controlling. Somehow, I grew more aware that I must change things about myself to prevent the silence. His silence and withdrawal terrified me. I could not reach him. I could not touch him. Alone in the silence, I cried the familiar tears of feeling unworthy, unwanted, and unloved. I reflected on the pain of that child; helpless as in that orphanage, and as frightened as in that hospital crib. I felt the rejection of a cultural family, the loss of companionship and friendship, and the void of not belonging.

His silence meant the return of those unhealed feelings. I know I never understood where he went - only that he went far away. I kept changing myself, hoping I could love him enough. I kept an ever vigilant watch for the signs of his withdrawal, while searching endlessly for more love. I hated the silence. I hated running after him, but I continued to run. I became satisfied with his mere return. No real explanation, no real understanding of what happened; only that I must be to blame and I must change more about myself. Until now, I never realized that he kept running away - back into the comfortable discomfort of the hole in his heart.

Seeing the moments of his insecurity reflected my own. Instead of acknowledging them; I denied their existence. Through my warrior dance, I conquered each obstacle, penetrated each barrier; until I began to believe that I was strong and invulnerable. I was always the one so together. Not even in my despair was there evidence of my weakness. Not even in moments of pain were there tears to cleanse my heart. Not even in days of confusion and insecurities were there cracks in my armor. I had learned long ago to keep those feelings safely tucked in my heart.

Within the safe confines of myself, I saw myself falling apart. While I was able to conceal much, there was nothing that I could hide from myself. I saw it all too clearly. I had always been in control; and suddenly I was faced with what I had done to myself and with what I had allowed him to do. I became scared of myself and scared of him too. Afraid of the feelings I felt. Afraid that I would never return home. Afraid that losing him would be losing me too. Afraid that the familiar desperation of ending my life would this time be final and complete. Most of all, I was afraid of me - of the power of my spirit, of the power of my love, of the power of being ...

I ran for the final time back into the relationship where it was safe for me to hide and where I could be consumed by his needs and the many roles I took on to support them. Not realizing that I could never meet those needs. Not realizing that love would never be enough. Not realizing that I was helping to cage our spirits and that the longing to be free would grow feverishly as survival instincts must of necessity do.

I would have stayed there forever. It was so comfortable and comforting that I embraced the familiarity as peace and security. I relinquished any desires to aspire to the greater heights that my spirit wished to soar. The risk was too great, the loss immeasurable. Strange, how I knew that our marriage could not survive our own freedom to be. Without question, without hesitation, I would have stayed forever.

And then "she" came into our lives.

How she came into our lives, I am unsure. I cannot describe the gut-wrenching, soul-rendering devastation that permeated every ounce of my being. The devastation was complete. Every layer of my existence had been pillaged; and as a result, I found myself drowning in a whirlpool of the void where I saw my emotional body writhing in the pain of trust and love betrayed. I saw my intellectual body as it stumbled and made dazed attempts to comprehend the incomprehensible act of infidelity. I saw the stillness of my physical body collapsed and semi-conscious; exhausted by the weight of the strong, immortal image. Lying next to a well-worn shield was my warrior spirit, disarmed, tormented and anguished. The sight of my ever-present spirit wounded and still, brought the tears from the deepest caverns of my whole existence. From the bottom of my heart I stared, looking skyward through the opening of my hole and knew that there was no one left to heal the wounds. There was only me ... unsure, afraid, and broken.

This time, I did not run. I remained in my gaping wounded hole and began the slow painful healing I had long ago denied myself. Because of this final betraya l and my choice to stay, I emerged whole, healthy, and at peace with myself and the world. Because she came into our lives, I, in my solitary pain, finally chose to learn the love of self, of self-acceptance, and approval. I found worthiness and a sense of belonging. I reclaimed and integrated my feminine and masculine power and redefined my cultural identity. I learned to let go of him. My search for self ended, the circle complete. I arrived home where I began almost forty years ago.

Every day now, my spirit soars. It is free at last. With complete trust and knowledge that all things are possible, I dare to be me.

TWO

UNDERSTANDING THE HOLES IN MY HEART

Chapter 6

The healing began to happen when I entered the discomforting stillness of the void within the hole in my heart. Each time I ran away outside of myself, I learned only that it was imperative to erect additional barriers, impenetrable walls to keep my pain and vulnerability safely tucked away from anyone who would cause me more pain. This need to protect myself became one of my survival skills; and while it served me well, there was little, if any, evolution of my being.

It is more common to look outside ourselves for the resolution of conflict. It allows us to focus on challenging, external, tangible obstacles while assigning responsibility to them for the existence of our own fears and insecurities. Each of us is taught at a very early age that love, belonging, and a sense of significance comes from somebody else. As an infant cries from hunger or discomfort, a parent interrupts his or her own activity to provide nourishment for that infant. The nourishment is multi-dimensional.

The physical body is fed and hunger dissipates. Simultaneously, the infant feels safe and comforted; and most importantly, the infant feels significant and worthy of the nourishment. The sense of significance is attached to the presence of that parent and is perceived as nourishment ... physical, emotional, and spiritual.

As this infant grows into childhood, the need for the same nourishment does not diminish. Instead, it grows within this being and the concept that self-significance and worthiness comes from external sources is reinforced as it is daily given and withdrawn.

Trauma is as it is perceived by anyone. Since my attachment began as a process outside of my being, and because the results of such attachment were so fulfilling to me, I learned to yearn for more and more. It was the same good feeling, the same security, the same significance I looked for and needed from any relationship I entered. It was also the unfulfillment of these needs that resulted in the holes in my heart.

I am not attempting to assign blame or guilt to the unfulfillment of our necessary nourishment. Because trauma is perceived by each individual, it is simply the way it has occurred for many of us.

The circumstances of my early childhood were not designed nor desired by my parents. Their lives together began as many; conceived with the dreams of love and the vision of life together. They are not responsible for what I perceived as trauma. The events simply happened. For example, their inability to be there when I needed them was not of their own choosing. They made whatever right choices they could given the external conditions which existed and options available to them. It was my interpretation of those unmet needs which became trauma for me. I made that determination based on whatever external messages I received during that immediate moment in time where my "hunger" for nourishment existed.

We have all experienced those moments in time. These moments are real and valid. They cannot be compared to any other ... for there can be no greater trauma than another. Unfortunately, one of the ways to validate our feelings is by making our own trauma larger and more devastating than someone else's.

This is a result of a lack of awareness and acceptance of our own pain. I remained in the intellectual awareness of "nobody's fault," "they did the best they could," and "I survived it, so what's the big deal" many times in my life. This detachment allowed me to survive the painful trauma and to continue my life's journey. As a survival skill, it was extremely successful. This detachment also allowed for the acknowledgment of perceived trauma without having to feel the feelings caused by trauma. It allowed me to deny or to devalue those feelings as serving no useful purpose. It enhanced my self-image as a strong, capable warrior.

This is a wonderful pay-off for remaining detached. The lost, frightened vulnerability of that little girl need never be addressed by me as long as I continued to stay busy slaying the external dragons around me. It is little wonder that entering the void is so terrifying. Many of us do whatever is necessary to prevent this from happening. Entering the void means seeing those fears clearly. It means standing absolutely still while confronting personal dragons of insecurities; but most of all, it means feeling those feelings again. For only when we acknowledge them, can we let them go. Only when we know why they exist, do we know why we cling tightly to them. Only when we feel the loss of letting them go, can we know the hole that exists within us. Only when we feel the emptiness of that hole can begin to fill it. Entering the void is the running inward toward the hole rather than denying or devaluing its existence. It is the beginning of healing.

Emulating my first hero, I spent my earlier warrior days playing war much in the ways I imagined my father battled the "real" enemies of the "real" army. Every playground became an opportunity to fight for truth, justice, and the "American Way. " I sought out experiences that would allow this warrior to fight the external circumstances which I held responsible for the first hole in my heart. I became the advocate for the less athletically inclined; always choosing the children no one wanted on their team. I challenged the bullies and the arrogance of those who thought themselves to be better than the rest of us. I never knew whether they really believed they were better, it didn't matter then. It was their external action that I reacted to. I could only see the relief on the faces of those "unchosen-before" kids and could feel the happiness of their belonging. They belonged; so I did too.

Because I learned that both the fulfillment and unfulfillment of nourish-ment exists outside myself, this kind of "warrior-ing" was both natural and gratifying to me. I learned to fulfill my needs by taking care of others. What I did not realize was that I had redefined my own needs for nourishment. As a result, the time would come when I wanted my turn "to be taken care of " and no one would be available. Because my concern for others outweighed my concern for self, I had literally made it impossible for anyone to take care of me. I began at an early age to feel the self-sabotage effects of being the "world's mother."

So on we go; bloodied and battered, fighting one dragon after another with but a single mission.

The older I grew, the more skilled I became in my warrior role. Time would see me fighting for civil rights, women's rights, and human rights. Always a battle, always strategizing, always looking outside to change the external environment so that I would not feel the feelings lying safely in my heart. They were, and still continue to be, positive reinforcement for this warrior spirit. That is why so many of us run with this spirit, seeking others of similar causes. How noble and selfless we are viewed by others and consequently, their approval can fill some empty place within us. So on we go; bloodied and battered, fighting one dragon after another with but a single mission. If everyone can be just and fair with the same truth, then we may just get what we need to feel significant, worthy, secure, and loved once more.

The warrior's battles are many. They are also time-consuming. Days are filled with a constant thirst for knowledge; with activities that cultivate and refine the skills of strategy, of tactics, and counter-tactics. There is little time for rest and consequently there is a compulsion to nourish the physical body as well as the intellectual body for the endurance required of life-long battles.

I developed a keen sense of vision; able to grasp the overall concepts of social structure; to identify the "haves" and the "have-nots." I learned the power of structure and could anticipate the use of the system to rape and pillage the masses. I understood how to go underground and to work with quiet resistance when necessary, and when to wage an all-out assault. Both constant preparation and actual battle necessitate a detachment of feeling. There was genuine compassion and empathy for others; but little time or need for the same compassion toward myself (or so I thought).

The song of the warrior is the "us against the world" melody. It is founded on overcoming trauma; but more importantly, its tune was composed by scarcity Not enough to go around. Not enough love or attention. Not enough places to belong. Not enough nourishment ... physically, emotionally, or spiritually. This scarcity manifests itself in a multi-dimensional way and is reinforced in our external world. As long as we continue to look outside ourselves to meet our needs, we continue to maintain our attachment to others in ways that continually deny the fulfillment of those needs. Each attachment brings another hole in our heart.

Chapter 7

Because I experienced moments of being unloved or abandoned by someone else, I clung to any thread of love since moments of love from someone were better than nothing from no one at all. Because I experienced the hunger of not having enough food and material possessions, I clung to the same, however little they might be. Something was better than nothing at all. Because I experienced the loss of faith in others, I clung to the spiritual symbols of faith wherever I found them ... for temporary solace was better than no comfort at all. Our external world always provides for the necessity to hang on to these attachments. When we look around us, we see that love can only be of value when it exists within a relationship. Our truth and our message of what love is becomes the completion of the whole.

Love is filling the emptiness of the void of loneliness. It is the comfort and the security of being connected to another. It is the knowingness of sharing a path with another which brings the freedom and courage to spread one's wings. It is the anchor; the roots of a beginning, firmly implanted in the common needs of another; thus, allowing a being to evolve without losing touch with the earth. It is the pleasure of the giving of one's self freely in exchange for the gift of belonging. It is the euphoric warm glow of being loved and acknowledged as a priceless gift from the heavens above from one unique and priceless being to another equally unique and priceless being.

I found comfort in the masses whose unquestioning faith in external philosophies allowed for moments of peace and respite from the turmoil of conflict.

It is the growing and evolving into one another. It is the merging of wandering spirits creating security and comfort for unfilled desires and needs. It is the resulting oneness that is perfection. It is the oneness that is empowering; and the quiet knowingness of shared strength and energies to travel life's mountains and valleys.

It is the embodiment of pleasure, joy, and the unselfish giving of mind, body, and soul that allows both spirits to soar together ... enhancing the oneness ... ever evolving into each other. This external message of love is that love is of value when there is the merging of two separate beings creating one relationship, one identity, and one set of needs and wants.

We also learn that in order to make a difference in this world, we need to be heard. In order to be heard, we must be in a position of perceived power. We learn that our physiological needs must be met in order to pursue what is right and just. If I am without food or shelter, then am I a credible voice of truth? If I relinquish my hold on the smallest o fmaterial possessions, because there are so many without; is it conceivable that those possessions will be taken from me? The less I have, the more I fear I will lose. Because this is a fear left unacknowledged, I can only chastise those I perceive who have more. Because I perceive they have more and our external world applauds the "having more," the "having more" becomes being more. I do not want to be less, so I hang on.

In my moments of trauma when there was hopelessness or helplessness, I seach for a way out of this discomfort. I had no answers or explanations for these feelings of betrayal and despair. My search led me to a faith beyond myself. I found comfort in the masses whose unquestioning faith in external philosophies allowed for moments of peace and respite from the turmoil of conflict. Because I was not alone, as when I endured the betrayal of faith; I confused the comfort of others as the comfort of these philosophies. For many, it is unthinkable to accept that these philosophies cannot provide the answers to the emptiness of our holes.

Each of these dimensions of clinging consume every level of our being with such intensity that we fully embrace them as real and fulfilling. While we are nourished, the nourishment is temporary; because all things, people, and places in our lives are not permanent. This reliance upon external gratification of needs sets us up to fall again and again. Each time we fall, we enlarge the hole in our hearts. Each time we must find something, someone or someplace bigger and better to help us feel better. We become trapped in our own external worlds.

So it is for many of us who continue to search for just the right person, just the right thing, just the right faith, to make us feel whole and complete. When we are unable to feel whole and complete, when we think we have lost the missing piece, our external world withdraws its support and the message is either we wanted or expected too much, or we did something wrong. Either way, we feel less than, inadequate, unworthy, unsupported, and unloved. The circle is complete. We begin our definition of self outside ourselves and we redefine the same self from external messages we receive.

It is the completion of this circle that leaves the warrior without a place or method to do battle. Every effort has been thwarted and every alternative becomes another obstacle. It is a time of great loss. Old strategies, old messages, and old beliefs are unworkable and unbelievable. It is at that moment we feel that we no longer have anything left to lose. We are left alone in the doorway of our own void.

Chapter 8

I checked and re-checked the luggage. One final look around the house. Off to another Air Force adventure. We were leaving the tiny, humid, tropical island without hesitation or reservation. I was looking forward to a new direction in career and an opportunity to enjoy the much talked about beauty of the Hawaiian Islands.

Resolving the abrupt end to a job was different and difficult this time. The staff had become more than co-workers ... they were family. Several of us had orders; and this family of professionals would never again experience the kind of esprit de corps that we enjoyed. It was time, too, to leave line staff counseling work. I wanted to do something that could reach more people. I had a tremendous volunteer staff. Together we were successful and effective working with the issue of family violence. It was now time to move on.

I learned much about myself and professionally I felt capable and confident in ways I had not felt before. There was a part of me that wanted to hang on to what we had accomplished. There would be tremendous changes in that service. But change in staff necessitates change in direction. Difficult as it was, I accepted that. It was far more difficult for the volunteer staff I left behind.

Putting aside those sad thoughts, I returned to the last minute details of leaving. This was th e first time that I held no resentment toward him. His job would uproot us again; but this time, I looked forward to a new direction in our lives. Life together was far better than life apart.

These two balck women stood in front of me, tears in their eyes. "He's having an affair with "B."

All time came to a screeching halt. In one split second, there was absolute stillness as I struggled to regain my composure.

These two women had been on my staff. Their sincerity and discomfort, obvious, as they struggled with their anxiety over my immedite response. There was none. Part of my cultura l heritage is to display no emotion. Part of me in the hole in my heart learned to keep emotions safe.

"She" was a young, white woman on my staff. She had entered our lives slowly and had spent many hours in our home befriending everyone from house- keeper to my daughter. She viewed me as her mentor and many hours were invested in nurturing her professional growth.

Numbly, I brought these two messengers of truth into the bedroom as we waited for him to return with the airline tickets.

"Yes, it is true." He stood there, so calm, so together. He too, had learned to hide his emotions. There was more silence. I calmly walked these two messengers to the door and thanked them for the difficulty of their task. We said our final good- byes. I slowly turned and walked back to the bedroom.

A thousand thoughts bombarded my brain simultaneously. I looked at him. I saw nothing. I felt the anger surge and the hurt well within me. I fought for control. I could not break now. I would not.

There were many times in the past years that I had had doubts. The times he didn't come home. The late night phone calls. A letter sent to my office. I had dismissed the doubts as my own insecurities which he confirmed. I wanted to believe him, and I chose life together - again and again. After all, he had often been moody and withdrawn. He needed his space and I wanted him to have it. No matter what happened, I knew that he would never do anything t ohurt me. So the believing was easy. I changed more about myself so that the doubts would disappear.

Now, everything dissolved into that one moment of truth. Now, I knew nothing. I hated that I could never know how many times before. I hated myself for so blindly loving him that I could make such wrong choices. I hated that moment for its ugly, gnawing truth. I ran into the bathroom. My body shook violently and I wretched uncontrollably.

I felt completely violated. There was no part of my being where I could run for refuge. So I stood there, looking at myself in the mirror and knew that I was undeniably lost and alone.

Then came the barrage of questions. When? How long? What happened? Why her? My staff, my office, my personal place? My job was all that was mine alone . It mattered that she was white. It mattered that the messengers were black. My cultural identity was assaulted again. My sexuality was raped again. My emotions were pillaged again. My faith in myself, my judgment, my choices were all subject again. The ultimate betrayal of friendship. For this main was the only human being on this earth who knew more of the pain in my life, more of my fears, and more of my struggles. This man, who quietly entered my life at a time when I had no faith in lasting relationships, had given me faith in "love." This man, more than any other person, I would have died for. This man had just done the unthinkable.

Alone that night, unable to contain my anguish any further, I sobbed. The pain flooded the hotel room. I cried for us. I cried for him. I cried for myself, mostly for myself. I cried for all the tears that had been safely hiding for 35 years.

All the feelings, all the fears, all the events of my life suddenly burst within my being.

Suddenly, I wanted to make love. I wanted to have something to hang on to. I wanted the pain to go away. I wanted to run into my physical body. As we cried and tried, I knew then that not even my body could respond to the complete devastation of my being.

It was the moment I found my whole being ... emotional, mental, physical and spiritual bodies ... collapsed in the doorway of my own void. With nothing left to lose, I entered the void and welcomed the absolute stillness.

Throughout my lifetime, when faced with trauma, I retreated quietly and momentarily within myself; long enough to find a new alternative, a new strategy, a new survival technique to cope with the hardships the trauma presented. When

It was the moment I found my whole being ... emotional, mental, physical, and spiritual bodies ... collapsed in the doorway of my own void.

the feelings hurt too much, I stopped feeling by concentrating on developing my physical body. When my body was assaulted, I relied on my mental skills. When I lost faith in the outside world, I developed an unshakable faith in myself. Those lessons came as a result of the confrontation and analysis of the present event, its meaning, and perceived solutions. This time, however, was quite different in the depth of pain, depth of questioning, and subsequent depth of understanding. Rather than to simply withdraw inward, I found myself fully in the midst of what I perceived to be a bottomless, endless void.

The void is the confrontation of the total self by the total self. It is the re-experiencing and the relearning of all perceived truths. It is the self stripped of all external thoughts, feelings, and messages. And it is the total comprehension of those thoughts, feelings, and messages. It is a place of whole healing. It is both an ending and a beginning. The lessons are personal, yet they are also universal. It is the message of the void that is the healing song for each of us.

I recognize now that we enter the void many times in our lives and if we choose to accept the answers within, we emerge with greater understanding of ourselves and others. The circle of personal growth is spherical - so that we may arrive at many familiar lessons again and again to gain greater understanding, growth, and peace. Whatever event triggers our entrance into the void is merely a catalyst for our learning. Our stay in the void is dictated only by what we choose to learn. For the next three years, I would live life from within my own void.

Deep within the hole in my heart, beyond the fears and pain, beyond the anger and frustration, beyond the seemingly endless tears, lay the path to freedom. Deep within the hole in my heart, I found and fell in love with myself.

Chapter 9

The mountains of Hawaii soared into the clear blue sky. They stood tall, displaying the wonder of their creation. Never had I seen anything of such awesome beauty. Never had I experienced the depth o f such wonder as I greeted them daily. Seeing the way they abruptly emerged from the earth's surface reminded me of the current path I was traveling.

Arriving in Hawaii, I yearned for something familiar to hold on to. I was still deep within my pain, every part of me hurt. Like the mountains' sudden emergence, being in the void was like suddenly, abruptly being thrust into another world. I had no place to land.

The brilliant blues and greens of the ocean brought the only moments of the soothing comfort I longed for. The roar of the waves thundered in my mind like the roar of all of the difficulties in my life. As they crashed against the rocks, I was both humbled and intimidated by the power and force of each wave. Several currents surged together with their own power and energy. The resulting impact was deadly; much like I imagined the effects of my own anger.

Yet, in spite of this power, the waves gently receded from those same rocks with soothing and cleansing compassion. Like the surge of the different currents, waves of my emotional being from many directions in my life culminated in one crashing blow against the holes in my heart. I prayed for the comfort of the gentle cleansing of those rocks below me. I began to tentatively hope that even as I experienced the depth of my emotions, my releasing them would also cleanse my anguished heart.

As I sat perched on the cliffs high above the thundering waves and the well-worn rocks below, I began to embrace each wave of emotion.

As I sat perched on the cliffs high above the thundering waves and the well-worn rocks below, I began to embrace each wave of emotion. Expressing the intensity of these emotions was extremely frightening. It was the fear of my own anger expressed that had prevented me from letting it go. Yet, I knew that the time and place to stop running was here.

I realized that I never really expressed anger at the time that I felt it. Somewhere along the way, I learned that anger was an unacceptable emotion. Anger caused pain, violence, and self-destruction. As a young girl, I learned that anger was a statement of aggression. Later as a woman, I learned that it was also a character flaw in a personality. This myth was reinforced around me so much that I had made this myth a truth.

I began to see why I sought permission to be angry by the same masculine system that sanctioned anger. I perceived the expression of anger as an exclusive right of masculinity. In seeking permission from them, I denied my own right to be angry or to express it at the time I felt it. In seeking permission I also devalued the feminine system that by gender, I belonged to. The feminine world, by its silence, gave passive consent to this truth. Even now, at a time when I felt angry, I continued to question my right to be angry ... by waiting. I waited for his permission to be angry. I was waiting for a chance to express my anger at what he had done. But he was so pitifully remorseful, so self-denigrating that once again my compassion for him outweighed my compassion for myself. I found it difficult to lash out at someone who was doing such an effective job of self-abuse. I waited for my turn ... it never came.

Instead, inwardly I got angrier. The anger began to move into rage as I watched him leave to meet her. In his remorse, he wanted to tell her in person that he was sorry that he had led her on. He wanted her to know that, after all, he never intended to leave me. I felt abandoned. My feelings were discounted. Still, I did not express the anger. I think now, that I was afraid that expressing all of that anger would force him away and I was not prepared for that consequence. I let him go. Part of me understood his need to confront the fantasies he felt partly responsible for creating. That compassion and empathy for him gave him permission to leave, while at the same time, denied expression of my own anger. Instead of being angry with him, I became angry with myself.

It was self-directed anger that allowed me to see clearly how long I had been waiting to be angry. It was then that I realized that I must give myself permission to be angry. This remorseful man, and the masculine system he was a part of, would never give me permission to be angry. I realized that by seeking permission, I was actually seeking acceptance of that anger and of many other feelings I was experiencing. How could I expect anyone else to accept my feelings, when I could not accept them?

I had run away from expressing anger a long time ago. Looking at the traumatic events of my life, I saw that when I felt overwhelmed by the injustice or unfairness of an event, my anger served only to add to my feelings of helplessness. The event appeared too enormous to change and anger made me feel out of control. Since I could not control the external turmoil, I learned to suppress the anger which gave me some sense of control.

To reinforce the need to suppress anger, patriarchal authority not only discouraged anger, but penalized women for their expression of it. The penalties ranged from humoring or discounting the feeling to attacking the personality of women by labelling them as aggressive, domineering, bitter, hostile, resentful "bitches." I wonder if men were as threatened by the possibility of female anger as women were threatened by the reality of male anger. Perhaps it was that "threatening feeling" that necessitated the patriarchal system to deny female anger.

Together, both internal and external messages led to the need to ask permission to be angry. I knew that I could no longer deny my own anger and I began to release it; however, not without consequences.

My anger was not met with sympathy, compassion, or understanding. It was met with his anger. He became angry that I was angry. Everything I feared would happen, happened. He withdrew. He counter-attacked. He rejected any validity of that anger. Yet, as the lid came off my bucket, the anger continued to spill until it was spent. It was then, that I began to let go. I was beginning to let go of the many roles I had taken on as appropriate and acceptable. I was beginning to let go of the external belief system that no longer suited my personality. I was beginning to redefine myself. I continued to let the anger come. The anger allowed me to move forward in my quest of self-awareness. I found a way to use my anger for self-discovery. I was no longer afraid of my own anger. I felt empowered by it.

Chapter 10

A consequence of anger denial and the belief of external messages of "appropriate" emotional display is the creation of dualistic thinking within a relationship. In moments of unexpressed anger, hurt, fear, or insecurities, I found myself questioning the validity of these feelings. I realized how frequently I made myself wrong. Being wrong helped me to continue holding on to unexpressed anger. Being wrong meant I could continue to look outside myself for answers to questions, for solutions to problems, for definition, and validity of me. In making myself wrong, I had made him right. I had always made him right.

Dualistic thinking exists within most relationships. Discussions, feelings, situations, and people are either right or wrong. Externalized messages create the rightness of men or male characteristics ... logical, practical, analytical, precise, linear thinking. Characteristics unlike these are devalued and imply "wrongness."

Where had I learned to be wrong? I had never received a direct message that I was wrong. It was always implied. The implication of wrongness happened many times in my life.

I learned at three, that there was a right color which was white; and a wrong color which was black. Wrong colors are treated with less fairness. Later, I learned that even within the wrong color, there is a color more wrong. Within this culture I had identified myself with, there were definitions of being black enough. There existed the perception that being of lighter skin color meant one was less "black." I also learned that being multi-cultural meant being confused about my identity. These messages were reinforced by the rejection of my heritage and the direct messages of not being black enough.

I learned the wrongness of emotional display as a child every time I was chastised and punished by my father, my mother, the nuns, and every time I watched it happen to others. I learned the wrongness of being a girl because boys had more choices, more freedom to challenge, to take risks. I learned that being female was a larger crime than rape itself, for I had made the wrong choices at the wrong time with the wrong person.

Even now, because I had made him right, part of me felt wrong for wanting him to stay with me. Later, after the dissolution of our marriage, there would be many others as well as he that would find it necessary for their own acceptance to know what or who was wrong. I would be held responsible for having made him right and punished for any truth or display of anger. It would be easier to be blamed. After all, he was right, which made me wrong.

When we create dualistic thinking within the relationship, the wrong person has wrong expectations and needs, as well as wrong feelings. A paradox exists in my expectation that only the "right" person can fill the holes in my heart. Any attempt to fill my own holes is inadequate and wrong because I am wrong. Yet, because the holes are my own, no one will ever be able to heal them and the needs continue to exist unmet.

It was the release of anger that allowed me to see that I was not wrong. I did not create the painful feelings because I deserved them. I had chosen to believe the implied wrongness of my being.

With building excitement, I began to feel the power of my choices. If I had chosen to believe I was wrong and I had chosen to create his rightness; unquestionably, then, I could choose to create my own rightness without creating wrongness.

I also began to realize that in my wrongness, I not only sought permission to be angry or to be right; I sought forgiveness and therefore approval and acceptance of my self. I forgave myself for waiting because I now understood why I waited. I forgave myself for feeling, for believing, for living the many roles I had chosen to live. I forgave myself for not being whatever anyone else thought I should be or needed me to be. I forgave myself for making all the choices I made because I now understood that every choice was the best choice I could have made at that time. I understood also, that

... I began to believe that I could heal myself. With that, I stepped into the first rays of light emanating from within the hole in my heart.

making one choice is not irrevocable. I had the right to make new and different choices at any time I needed to. I needed only to give myself permission and to assume the responsibility for those decisions. Through my forgiveness of myself - I gave away "wrongness."

When I decided to stop looking outside myself for answers, for validation, for all of the people, places, and things to heal my wounded self; I began to believe that I could heal myself. With that, I stepped into the first rays of light emanating from within the hole in my heart.

Chapter 11

Choosing self, choosing to honor the self, and choosing to accept all of my feelings opened the door of my cage. Through the door, rushed the innumerable possibilities of life. Within me many new thoughts and perceptions began to grow. I was exhilarated with the accompanying freedom of choices; I was not able to fully grasp or to revel in my new evolution. Confusion and conflict also existed within me. It seemed I was on an unending roller coaster. With the freedom to choose, came the fear of choosing.

I found myself constantly questioning one "old" truth after another. Having no frame of reference for the new, it was difficult at first to grasp the new way of feeling or thinking without having to confront the old way.

It was only the growing discomfort of the old way that pushed me forward. There was no logical, practical, analytical, or tangible way to validate this newly chosen path. All the external messages remained the same. This caused an increase in conflict within my significant relationships. The conflict made me afraid because there was a sense of impending loss. I wasn't sure that I wanted to lose anything anymore.

When we expect others to fill our needs, emptiness, or sense of self, codependency develops and fear of loss is the result. Codependency can happen in any relationship. While people in codependent relationships appear close, they are in fact much closer, they are attached. So attached are they, it is often difficult to see where one begins and ends. When attachment like this exists within, it is so strong that children of these relationships must learn codependent attachment whether or not it meets their initial needs.

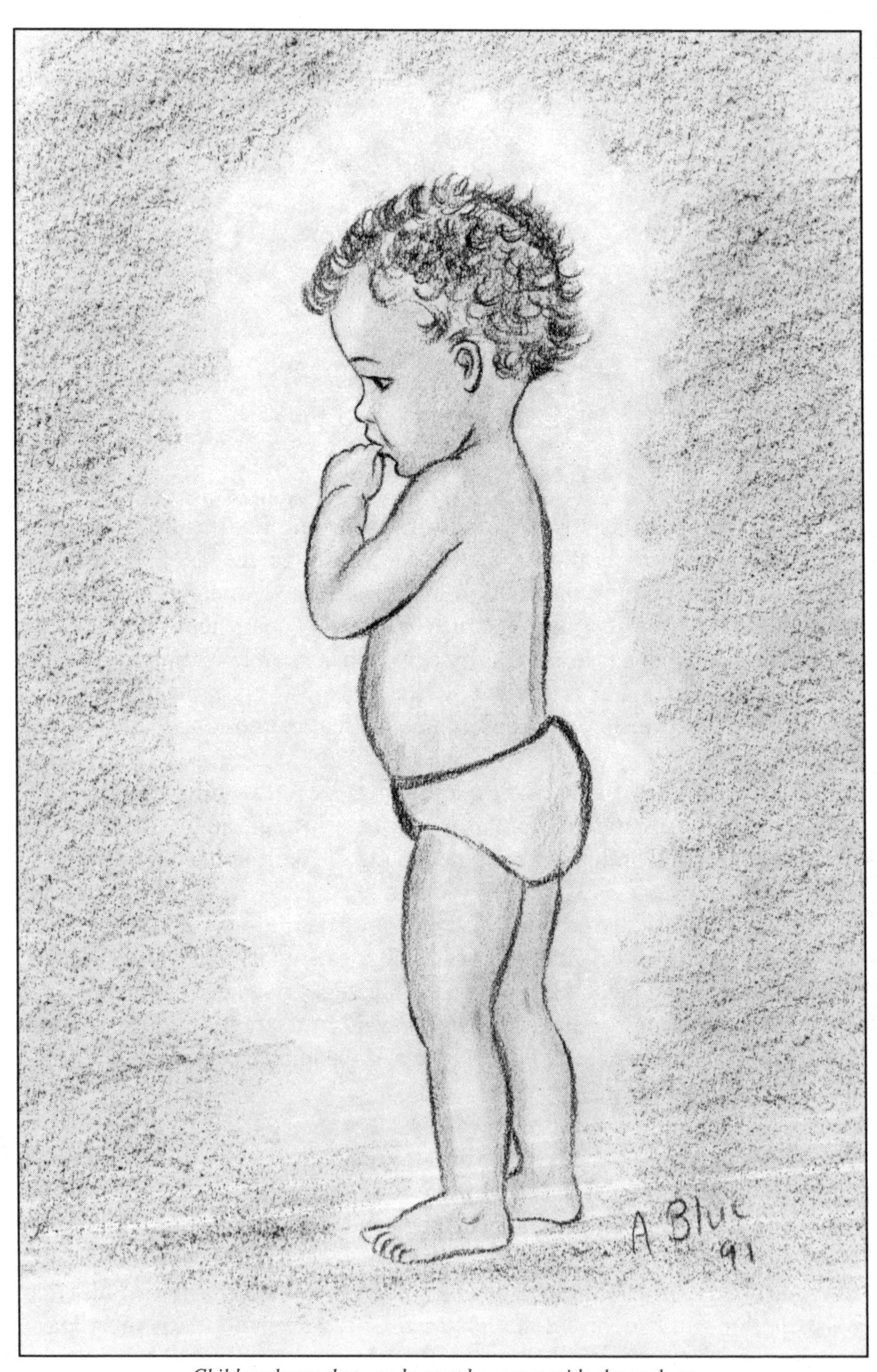

Children learn that needs must be met outside themselves.

Children learn that needs must be met outside themselves.

I have spent ten years counseling men and women in abusive/addictive relationships. I have seen the degree of attachment that exists within these relationships. The fear of loss is often so great that it overwhelms the fear of being hurt. Because no one has the capability to meet the total needs of another, the attachment grows stronger. What I was beginning to discover was that this attachment did not exist exclusively within abusive relationships. It exists in almost every relationship because we are all part of a greater system which teaches, encourages, and supports externalized methods of meeting needs.

Attachment relationships require the parts of another in addition to the parts of self to create a whole being. The stronger the attachment, the smaller the part of self becomes. Children in these codependent relationships are never really given an opportunity to become whole. They emulate only what they perceive is appropriate from the adults they are completely dependent upon. Adults find it difficult to break the attachment because the greater system does not support non-attachment or individualized boundaries.

Another result of a codependent family is the tansference of dependency from one being to another. Imagine a family of parasites. When one person is unable to provide the lifeblood for the survival of another, there is always someone else available to use untilthe supply is replenished. It is the insidiousness of this transference that makes breaking attachments so difficult and fearful. The questions of whose problems is whose, or whose needs or whose feelings are as intertwined as the people themselves.

Breaking codependency in these relationships induces a tremendous fear of loss. Because there must be a letting go of all attachments, the part of self that remains feels overwhelmed by fear, helplessness, and emptiness. Because the attachment is so entrenched, every thought, feeling, or action becomes solely dependent on the thoughts, feelings, or actions of another. The ability to trust the self is significantly diminished. This increases the fear of loss. Breaking attachments of codependency leaves the self solely dependent upon the self which it does not know or trust.

It was painful to recognize that I had chosen to live my whole life based upon my father's thoughts, feelings, actions, and reactions. It was painful to recognize that I had chosen to live my marital life the same way based also upon my husband's thoughts, feelings, actions, and reactions. It was painful to acknowledge that this betrayal left me without even a crumbling foundation. Since I had centered my life around my husband, I could not rebuild the same foundation without setting myself up to fall again. It was painful to accept the level of my attachment.

It was only when *the pain of attachment outweighed the fear of loss* that I was able to re-examine my fears and to re-establish trust in myself. The process was not easy, but feeling the pain rather than denying it moved me onward.

I chose to feel the pain, to feel the fear, and to do it, anyway. I had nothing to lose. I knew that I was not living life - I was merely surviving. Surviving meant waiting. I chose to wait no longer.

Another underlying fear that makes breaking attachment so difficult is the fear of being alone. Our external world sends clear messages about the wrongness of being alone. Alone means unwanted, unloved, and unworthy. When I perceived myself as abandoned as a child, I took on these labels and feelings. Since someone could take away these feelings of loss, my aloneness would validate the social messages.

It was only when *the pain of attachment outweighed the fear of being alone* that I was able to embrace myself. Until now, I had accepted these externalized messages, regardless as to whether they were wholly comfortable or not. Until now, trust and belief in this outside world brought me confusion, frustration, pain, anger, wrongness, and fear. I realized that these were some of the things I would lose if I developed the same trust and belief in myself.

As I began to detach from the external world, my focus shifted from what I would lose to what I could gain. In my detachment, I began to see the flaws in my externalized way of thinking. I also say that this way of thinking had once served a purpose for me. It provided a sense of belonging. It was a blueprint for mass consciousness. As long as we are all following the same plan, then none of us ever has to confront the self. But because the blueprint is so rigid, most of us are unable to follow the same plan, the same way, or for the same amount of time. The fact that that occurs implies that the plan is not the sole truth or path each of us can blindly accept. Our sense of belonging or sense of whatever need was met initially can no longer be met in the old way. It no longer serves a useful purpose.

Realizing that I was hanging on to a belief which served no useful purpose made it easiser to let go. And as I let go of the old way, a new way replaced it. Therefore, there was no emptiness to fill.

Chapter 12

I had been asked the question only once before. It was time again to ask the question of myself. I began by asking, "What do I want?" It was not as difficult to answer this time. I had been living with fear of loss and hurt so long that the words glided easily from my soul. "I want peace. I want peace of mind, peace of heart, peace of body, and the serenity of soul." I realized also just how long I had wanted it. I had always wanted peace. It was what I was seeking to obtain in every level of my work, my relationships, and my life.

From within the holes in my heart, I came to see how the struggle to bring peace to others was not the only goal. The other goal was to bring peace to me. I looked around me and found in every person and every experience the reflection of a lesson I needed to learn. The clues were all around me. I was able to perceive these experiences as lessons for my soul because this time I looked out from within the holes rather than from outside them.

I had spent much of my life doing for others. I had been an activist for civil rights, women's rights, and human rights. I had developed a number of programs to assist in the empowerment of the oppressed. If all the world were at peace, then maybe I would be too.

I began to listen to myself as I spoke with my clients. It was incredulous to hear the power of my words as they were spoken. Where had they come from?

By withdrawing my efforts and expectations from the external world, I was able to let go of the fear of not having peace. When I lost the fear, peace appeared. I ralized then, that peace was within me all along ... I had simply given it away.

"I just want to be me," she said with great conviction. This beautiful young woman had taken on a military patriarchal system, challenging deeply entrenched rules and values with bloodied consequences. I asked her how long she was willing to continue battering herself.

Her answer was quite simple, "Until they get it."

"Get what? " I asked.

"Until they understand that I have feelings, that I am a human being. Just because they may outrank me, respect isn't automatic. As one human being to another, it has to be earned by the way we treat each other. So I refuse to accept it just because the rules say so."

"In other words," I said, "if they get it, then you'll get it! If they get it by accepting you, then you'll feel acceptance and approval for your being. If they get it by caring about you, then you will feel worthy of being cared about. If they get it by treating you with respect, then you can honor your being. If they get it, then you can also know that you were responsible for it and you can then fill the need to be needed and know why you exist. In other words, your whole sense of you, your purpose, your opinions, your thoughts, your actions, and feelings is dependent upon 'them' getting it."

My last questions were, "Well, how long have you been waiting for them to get it and how long are you willing to wait?"

Hadn't I done the same thing? How often had I witnessed this same battle among my colleagues?

She came into my life at the exact moment of my own questioning. This conversation mirrored my life to such an extent that while I wanted peace, I also expected it to be given to me. I began to understand that social transformation would not bring peace to each of us. As each of us found peace within, collectively, our world would be transformed and there would be peace among us. Like this young woman, I had been fighting the warrior battle for justice and while waiting, peace continued to elude me. By withdrawing my efforts and expectations from the external world, I was able to let go of the fear of not having peace. When I lost the fear, peace appeared. I realized then, *that peace was within me all along ... I had simply given it away.*

Like the birth of a butterfly as it emerges from its cocoon, I reentered the physical world.

Chapter 13

Like the birth of a butterfly as it emerges from its cocoon, I reentered the physical world. My vision and perceptions had been transformed while in the nurturing warmth of my cocoon. As I emerged, I took one tentative step after another, choosing to see the world from a higher plane. Rather than feeling apart from everyone and everything, I choose to begin my walk down a path that would lead me to feeling a part of the whole.

I began my walk by working with an issue that returned me to the first hole in my heart. From within my hole, I began teaching Inter-cultural Relations.

My sensitivity to the ever-present "ethnic background" information questions brought to the surface this society's value of categorizing, compartmentalizing, and labeling human beings. In every aspect of our society from employment applications to gift purchase questionnaires, this information is solicited. It is little wonder that many of us are reminded constantly that we do not belong.

Further, this concept of categorizing and labeling enforces a perception of all people, places, and things as adversarial. It is an "us" versus "them" philosophy. At any given time, whoever "us" is, our view of "them" is that "they" are not real, natural, normal, healthy, or good.

And if we begin the categorizing ethnically, other categories will be created: religious, sexual, educational, financial, age, experience, etc. The factions of belief systems exist solely for themselves without consideration or even acknowledgment of another except as it serves to reaffirm the "wrongness" or inferiority of that other.

It is little wonder we human beings find it difficult to accept one another. The society and its system which we created does not allow for acceptance.

Instead of being angry, frustrated and hurt, this time I chose to see myself, my mixed blood, my multi-cultural being as a bridge between these categories.

Clearly, I physically could belong to many categories. My perception of culture was an integration of many of the values associated with specific cultures. My insecurities and fears from past experiences were merely reflections of the fears and insecurities of a society which could not understand the differences of people. This lack of understanding and fear was both created and supported by the categorization and labeling of human beings.

To understand and subsequently to lessen the fear, there must be a change. A change of self-perception and a change of perceptions of others. It is far more comfortable and safer to remain in the hole of ignorance. We can remain there until *the pain of staying outweighs our fear and insecurities.*

Because I had never been able to fit neatly into one category or another, the pain has been mine all my life. I chose now to view myself as a bridge. I chose also the responsibility of educating those whose paths I crossed.

With compassion for their fears, I shared the message of cultural pluralism. Together we examined the myth of the "melting pot" theory and explored the possibility of other theories. In truth, the melting pot is an illusion that allows us as a society to deny the existence of racial separation.

To melt means to "dissolve" to "disappear gradually." If the definition of melt is applied to people, what is the message we are sending? If we melt some cheese into milk, then as the cheese loses its form and blends with the milk, we have created a new substance, which can be called cheese sauce. The milk also loses its characteristic features. Both ingredients lose their identity and take on another.

The illusion of the melting pot theory is that bringing together a variety of humans, each with unique characteristics, into one culture, creates a new culture and the elimination of labelling and categorization. Since this elimination does not exist within our present society, the melting pot theory also does not exist.

The melting pot theory is based on the premise of exclusivity. Characteristics of people who may resemble one another even vaguely, are dissolved into a greater culture. Those people of color, or characteristics who obviously differ are not included in the new mixture. This results in categorization. It involves a process of assimilation which means to absorb into the cultural tradition of another ethnic population or group. For those of us who do not fit into that other ethnic population, our perception is that we must give up or give away a part of our own identity. Many of us would not freely choose to give away part of our identity or part of who we are for the sake of a cultural category.

Consequently, the tendency is to cling tighter, sometimes with a fierce desperation to our own specific heritage and thus, we become as exclusive as the perceived "majority." It is understood that the underlying need is the protection and preservation of identity; however, the result is still the same. We are now "us" and they are "them. " Perceptions are further distorted by the reactive response to "us" by "them" as the distance between us continues to grow.

A theory that promotes inclusivity while allowing all of "us" to retain our own sense of who we are as the self defines it is called the *salad bowl theory*. The premise of this theory is that as a nation, we are culturally pluralistic. This theory allows that each of us is unique and of value and completely interdependent upon one another. Imagine a salad bowl containing a wide variety and limitless numbers of ingredients. Each ingredient alone has its own unique characteristics. Together, each ingredient retains this unique quality while experiencing the existence of other equally unique ingredients. Separately, tomatoes, lettuce, carrots, and broccoli are of value and worth as vegetables, but do not make a salad bowl alone. It is the combination of these ingredients which we refer to as a salad. Thus, interdependence is essential to the salad making. The example is not an attempt to over simplify an issue which is sensitive to us all. However, the solutions to institutionalized labeling and categorization need not be complex. Sometimes the difficulty merely exists in the resistance to change. Any change requires self-inspection, self-acknowledgment, and self-love. It is with these discoveries that the way is prepared for the acceptance and love of others.

Inclusivity brings together values that are shared by us all: honor of ancestors, security, success, loyalty to family, education, personal freedom, independence, loving, sharing, and caring. Inclusivity eliminates stereotyping. When we describe values, we describe ourselves. Since culture is a set of values and traditions, it has nothing to do with color.

Inclusivity precludes "selecting only one category, or one that closely resembles." It allows for individual choice and definition based on self-identification and comfort. It allows each of us to belong simply because we exist.

Healing takes place when each of us chooses to celebrate the "self " and gives permission to ourselves and therefore, to others - to label, categorize and compartmentalize as the self chooses.

By sharing the human values that are common to us all and by allowing my multi-cultural heritage to serve as a rainbow bridge, I allowed the healing of my own holes. Through my own healing, the resulting gifts became the tools of enlightenment for others. I began to see the blessings of the rainbow in all of us. The circle of my cultural identity was now complete.

I began this life as a human being free from labeling and free from categorization. This day, I returned to the freedom of being a simple human being.

Chapter 14

So excited by the inclusivity of culture was I, that I sought to bring this message into every endeavor I undertook. The bitterness, the helplessness, and the despair disappeared. In its place was the warm glow of joy, of peace, of a renewed gratitude for life itself. This new path was one that would lead to greater and higher truths.

I was asked to create, develop, and manage a shelter program for abused spouses and their children. This program would become a model for the Air Force because of its multi-dimensional, prevention-based philosophy. This program would come to be highly successful because of its implementation of inclusivity. It also served to complete many lessons for myself and to symbolize my evolution and healing as a spiritual being.

I had developed several shelter programs in the past so the task was familiar and although challenging, it was not difficult. What was different was me and that difference sometimes brought difficulty. It was difficult to cope with such a broad vision of what must be done. The old ways of handling crisis situations or of managing people would not fit into this vision. Doubts about implementing services based solely on instinct frequently surfaced. I was learning now to trust myself despite the roar of external messages or direction.

From the kitchen curtains to the crisis intervention, from the recruitment of volunteers to the community education workshops, the message was one of inclusivity. The program did not exist for "them," it existed for all of us. This reflected a shift in my own consciousness. It was urgent that the community take ownerships in this issue. Our families in need of help were as much a part

... the message was one of inclusivity. The program did not exist for "them;" it existed for all of us.

of the community as the helpers. We needed to help each other because we were interdependent and our goal was peace for all.

As a warrior, the relentless struggle for justice was also a relentless pursuit of a fulfillment of my own need. Because I had felt powerless, I wanted other oppressed peoples to have the power. The dualistic exclusive world we live in reminds us that if there are those who are powerless, there are those who are powerful. "Victimized" people are obviously powerless. As shelter programs emerged across the country, we sought to bring power to those victimized by advocating, legislating, and addressing the issue of family violence. As warriors for justice, it became a life-consuming mission for many of us. We strived to climb the mountain where the powerful live, to conquer them with the facts of the daily horrors with which millions of us live. No matter how high the mountain, no matter how fatigued the warrior ... the battle to preserve a sense of rightness, a sense of significance, a sense of belonging, and a sense of hope waged on. As warriors we knew that without our compassion, perseverance, and knowledge, these oppressed would forever remain "victims" of our exclusive world.

I became consciously aware that each of us is suffering from the holes in our hearts. These are the same holes of not belonging, of being wrong, of anger denial, of fear, of loss, of our need for significance, and our resulting attachment. Even those whom we perceive as "powerful" must experience some of the same fears and insecurities as they cling tightly to their "rightness" for fear of losing their power. It was from these common holes that I began to teach and communicate the higher message of empowerment. I realized that no one can give true empowerment. It comes from within the self.

True empowerment differs from the dictionary definition of empowerment which states "to give power or authority." This definition reflects a dualistic externalized way of thinking that encourages the "us versus them," "powerful versus powerless," " victim versus oppressor" roles present in our daily lives. To give power or authority implies one is in a position of having power and the other is in a position of needing it. No wonder, the less powerful feel the need to ask permission. No wonder we wait.

True empowerment comes from the acknowledgment of the self for its strengths as well as its weaknesses. It is the knowingness that as a being we can choose to perceive the self as strong, capable, loving, and fulfilling. It is the trust of the self, the willingness to rely upon the self without having to eliminate or to eradicate or to change another. It is the acceptance and approval of self which makes for acceptance and approval of others. It is an internalized way of living. It is living from the inside outward.

The shelter program served as a symbol of personal empowerment. Education, the food for the mental body, provided strength to clients, volunteers, and the community. Through education, we began to understand the complexities of family violence. We provided the same educational training to clients and helpers so that they would know and be able to articulate and label their own issues. By providing our own personal experiences of emotional pain, our understanding was enhanced by our mutual feelings. Each of us acknowledged that we knew fear, shame, guilt, love, hate, anger, and despair. Through our own acknowledgment, we found commonality with all. Sharing common feelings created a bond of understanding and true compassion. Coming from where everyone comes from - "the heart" - created a trusting, open environment which allowed for multiple choices for the clients. Their choices and opinions were valued and validated by the genuine empathy created from within our own heart connection.

Emotional inclusivity brought us compassion for ourselves and for everyone. Every aspect of shelter and outreach exemplified the spirit of humankind. Every staff member reflected the community in which we lived and for which we served. Men, women, young, old, service men or women, and children of all colors and philosophies were part of a joint effort to help one another. We all learned to grow, to change perceptions of ourselves, and to embrace the lessons our lives had presented to us. We learned to be stronger because of the broken places. For each lesson brought a deeper understanding of the self as we recognized that what the external world had defined as weakness was really a tremendous strength. We were all survivors of some trauma that produced the holes in our hearts. As a community, we were empowered by our commonality and inner strengths.

With a continuing thirst for knowledge, I chose to integrate anything and everything I read or experienced. I chose to open the program to implement tried and true techniques as well as non-traditional teaching. My new perspective allowed for the value and worth of all beings. Each person was a part of the whole for there was as much learning from our clients as there was teaching.

She came to us before the acute battering. Thirty-five years old, she had lived with the pain and fear of family violence for the fourteen years she was married to him. She had sought help before, but the command had appeared less than supportive. They had recently arrived in Hawaii. It had been several months since the last time. His first sergeant had recently completed our assessment and intervention training.

The family had attended a squadron picnic when the first sergeant became aware of her husband's growing belligerence. He intervened and spoke to both of them separately. She remarked how surprised she was at this simple gesture. She went on to say how knowledgeable he was about their problems. "It was like he was living in our house!" He went on to validate her fears and concerns while offering her the option of the shelter. He stressed that any decision must be her own and no matter what she chose, he would be supportive. He also told her that he would offer the same support and could provide a place where her husband could get help, too.

It was his calm, reassuring knowledge of the issue as well as his genuine concern that allowed her to make the decision to seek shelter.

Upon her arrival, she was greeted by a warm team of volunteers who provided hours of concerned listening and allowed her a safe place to be. They reinforced her choice for decision-making while providing the information that would assist her in making decisions. She was stunned to see the numbers of volunteers in and out of the shelter that weekend: men, women, young, and old. Some came with their own children as playmates for her children, giving her time to talk and time to be alone.

She was overwhelmed by the beauty of the home; each room sponsored and decorated by the men and women of various squadrons. For the first time, she realized that she did not have to walk alone.

For fourteen years, she had lived in an isolated world of physical pain and emotional anguish. For fourteen years, she believed that there was no way out. That day the smallest glimmer of light struck her heart.

Later, her husband would join a men's support group as she had joined a women's group. Together, week after week, they were taught a variety of ways to unlearn the destructive patterns of their lives. Under the watchful guidance and support of social workers, first sergeants, chaplains, and their peers, they began to apply their newly learned skills.

They celebrate each year of violence-free marriage as a gift they give to themselves and to each other. He went on to start support groups for other men using the information he was taught. She continues to work with other women. Together, they are on their way to a healthier life.

He continues to contribute to the Air Force mission as a worthy significant part of the whole. Only now he knows just how worthy and significant he is.

Without condoning the crime of violence, the community combined their wisdom, knowledge, and skill with their collective energies and created an environment that in this instance, led to her decision to remain in the marriage. That same effort enabled him to make significant changes in his behavior. Their willingness to share their "secret" allowed us to know more, to understand more, so that we could better serve another neighbor. Intuitively, I knew that our interdependence would speed the healing for all; if we could only come from where we all begin - in the hole in our hearts.

My reliance and trust in my inner voice grew daily. It was not long before every decision, every interaction, every daily activity was guided by my inner voice. It was the trust of myself that prompted me to share with others the joy of developing a trust in themselves. These "powerless" people had developed a keen sense of survival instincts. What they lacked was their awareness of their own power.

The success of this program grew in a phenomenal six months. Our reputation was far reaching as news travelled thousands of miles away from Hawaii to Washington, D.C. Many visitors and dignitaries sought a glimpse of what we had so effectively created. Together, inclusively, we were making a difference for all of us. The success of our combined energies continued to grow.

As it would happen, our light had beamed too brightly. As it often happens, new ways of thinking or being create fear and resistance in others, because it is not understood. No one ever knew the real reason, but the announcement came to close our House of Peace.

Chapter 15

There was such a deep wrongness about the closing of the shelter that was magnified by the covert, almost paranoid manner in which the decision makers handled themselves, the volunteers, the community, and each other. There was a greater wrongness that the closing symbolized. The hope, human spirit, and compassion which gently engulfed this community was betrayed by the politics of a dispassionate system which created it. The betrayal of hope was truly disheartening and painful to me and to the many others who had invested so much of themselves to the life work of service to others. For us and the many families left abandoned, there would never be a reason to justify the closing. None would ever really be given.

I looked deep within myself for the meaning of this lesson. I had lived as a "warrior" for such a greater part of my life that I could not fathom the reason for my lack of action.

Through my pain, I grew to understand the enormity of the work that needed to be done. I understood that while our success was overwhelming, it was also limited. What had been created was so right that many could benefit from thespecial gifts the program provided. If the program had continued, it would have continued toward a pattern of exclusivity and remained only a service for the few living in that small Air Force Hawaii community. I began to understand "the clinging to" that often happens when something is so wonderful and meaningful to another.

"Letting go" is a complex and painful lesson for us as humans. We are forever in search for the one special person, place or thing that can fill the emptiness within our hearts. Many of us search a lifetime, never really filling the hole completely; but always pursuing the one wish that would make up for the loss of wishes unfulfilled. If only we could understand and accept the abundance within our own beings; then we could also accept that joy, happiness, peace, and power come from within. "Letting go" is often a difficult concept to grasp because it implies an abruptness, a dropping, an ending of sorts. As I have discovered throughout my life, letting go is a process that can take place over a lifetime. It is part of an evolution of personal growth and leads to a greater understanding of self and clarity of vision. It is part of a process that allows healing to take place. It is also a process that allows depth of feeling for self and for others.

Because we are all taught lessons from an externalized system, we learn to look outside ourselves for answers to questions, for love and belonging, for security, and for peace and harmony. When we find what we perceive to be the answer to everything we are seeking, there is no simple enjoyment of the feeling at that one moment in time or space. Almost the instant we find it, we concern ourselves with how to hang on to it. It can be anything physical, emotional, intellectual or spiritual, as long as it is derived from external sources. Our deepest appreciation and gratitude is limited by the fear of losing it. Our moments become consumed with changing the self or changing others in our attempts to cling to something or someone that never really belonged to us. There is no ownership of people, places or things that is permanent.

Part of my discomfort of the shelter program was the carnival atmosphere that existed as the parade of curious dignitaries and visitors streamed through the facility. Though well intentioned, somehow I felt that the growing pride and possessiveness of this "model program" by the system's leadership misdirected the meaning of the shelter's existence. And perhaps that is why the decision to abandon the community was made without the true understanding of the consequences that would be felt by many. What existed within the program could not be tangibly seen or touched. Human spirit and compassion can only be felt and understood deep within the soul. They are intangible.

I believe that the decision-makers, to some degree, understood the power of empowered beings. From within their own fear came the callous and detached manner in which we were all treated. There was enormous fear and paranoia regarding any reactive or retaliatory response that might occur. What they could or would not understand is that through my pain, I chose to seek a higher vision of understanding of what was happening. I had moved through attachment to detachment to non-attachment. I had grown from a fear of loss to a quest for understanding.

Like many others, I found a sense of significance through my work. Much as I had earlier defined my sense of worth through relationships, I had shifted fulfillment of those needs to my work. I had, in essence, detached from my relationship with my husband because of the dysfunction of the relationship. Detachment happens when the unacknowledged feelings accumulate and there appears to be no resolution. It is a breaking of the attachment created by the search outside ourselves. Detachment is a time of feeling feelings minimally. Anger and resentment often aid in maintaining a detached position. It is both an offensive and defensive warrior strategy often triggered by some penetrating emotional wound.

To fight the warrior battle, the less intense the emotional feeling, the more effective the tactics become. Letting go while detached often leaves a larger hole in the heart. The loss is greater because vindictiveness and resentment are often part of the letting go. When the anger recedes, much destruction and hurt have taken place. Often the damage is irreparable.

I had learned earlier in life that my pain was intensified when I acted out of anger and fear. The consequence had almost cost me my life; so it was more difficult for me to sustain anger and resentment. I had chosen this time to use detachment as an opportunity to acknowledge, accept, and understand my inner feelings. In acknowledging my feelings, I had to accept the warrior part of me that wanted to fight to keep that program alive. I had a desire to fight for the collective consciousness of the community that had made such a difference for us all. I wanted to fight the ignorance and indifference of a system that had for so long, oppressed and victimized its people. I wanted to stop the institutionalized rape and pillage of the human spirit.

From a place of greater vision and an inner knowingness that there exists a higher purpose and greater reason for all things, I acknowledged those warrior thoughts and desires without making myself wrong for having them. Letting go without wrongness in this way allowed me to let go of the need to resist the change that was imminent.

Acknowledging the feelings and feeling the feelings without acting on them, is the non-attachment part of the process of true letting go. Detachment is the resisting of feelings and a need for acceptance of those feelings by someone else. Detachment enables acknowledgment and validation of the feelings and therefore of the self. If and when that validation occurs, then the self is given permission to let go. However, it is rare that the required depth of validation is ever given or received; and the letting go, under these circumstances, rarely happens without much pain and anger.

Letting go without wrongness of self also allowed me to eliminate blame. Like wrongness, blame serves no useful purpose other than to increase attachment and significance to external sources.

Though the closing of the shelter was wrong, the rightness was in the preservation of a gift which will serve a greater purpose. The closing was wrong only on one immediate level. The decision-makers were not to blame; their actions stemmed from a place of unawareness, fear, and resentment. Their perceived lack of compassion came from a place of detachment. It was what made the letting go easier for them. Perhaps it is also why no reason was ever given; the real reason was never understood.

I also acknowledged the shift of my unfulfilled needs to my work. I had grown attached to that service. Although I was successful, the attachment could only serve to prevent my own personal growth and evolution. I think now that whatever greater purpose and service I chose could not have been met without my own letting go of that attachment. In my aloneness, I was left to confront my own fears. This confrontation and acknowledgement propelled me further down my path allowing me to arrive at this place and time. I am now free to be and do what I choose to do without any fear of loss. What I have gained is a deeper, clearer meaning of my self and my life. Letting go of old ways, beliefs, and actions made room for newer, more productive ways. I have come to understand through the painful event of the closing of Our House of Peace that if I choose to handle pain by growing, that what appears to be loss is truly an immeasurable gain for the self.

The final farewell to the shelter and all it had symbolized was both painful and joyful. Remembering the many hours of love and labor spent there within that special place brought me tears. The faces of many women, men, and children were images eternally imprinted on the walls. Every room reflected the shadows of the holes in the hearts of those who sought peace and comfort in our home. Throughout the dismantling, we heard the echoes of laughter, of joy,

My healing heart and I walked away. Without another look back, I knew I had returned to myself.

and of hope renewed. We knew then that our work would continue. I knew at that moment that the very system I had been so attached to was the very system that I had been hiding in. The security and sense of belonging, the approval and acceptance I attributed to this system was a mythical gift I had created. I felt the magnitude of what I created and realized that I had done it all. The shelter and its philosophy had come from within my own heart and soul. It was time to walk away from the patriarchal system that for all my life I had longed to be a part of.

There was not a wrongness about this system; there was simply an awareness that this system was no longer needed by me. There was nothing left to prove. I realized that there was never really anything to prove in the beginning.

Walking away from the system, I brought many gifts from lessons learned. It was this masculine world that taught me how to fight the warrior battle using my intellect, my analytical, linear thinking. I learned law and order. I learned to lead with determination and perseverance. I learned to separate emotion from intellect, for the value of logic far outweighed the value of feeling.

Yet, I also learned from this final opportunity and challenge to create this program, that intellect alone brings a shallowness to the human experience. I learned to follow my intuition and to rely on my feelings when creating an environment that promoted the emotional healing of others. I learned the value of greater vision and higher lessons. I also learned that feeling the feelings and accepting them as good and worthy was a part of the evolution of personal growth. I have observed this system from a place of non-attachment and recognized the fear and pain of so many who have been entrapped in its all-consuming rigidity.

The time was here to walk away. As I walked away from the building, I noticed its cemented, impenetrable walls; a fortress built to withstand any warrior battle. I clearly saw the emptiness within; without the love, compassion, and human spirit, it was what this system had been all along. A skeleton of wishes, of needs, of the gaping holes in our hearts. One last glance. I felt the surge of the healing emotions, the hope of the human spirit, the compassion and love within my heart.

My healing heart and I walked away. Without another look back, I knew I had returned to myself. There would be no going back. The time had come to take the risk to go out on my own without fear, without hesitation. There was only a knowingness that at last my search for approval and acceptance was complete.

The joy of this gift to myself allowed me to walk away with peace and serenity. Our House of Peace was indeed a place for the empowerment of the self. It was a place for healing the holes in our hearts.

Chapter 16

The time had come to confront the unhealed wounds in my marriage. Just as I learned that approval and acceptance of my work came from within, I knew that fulfillment of my needs had to be redefined. *The pain of living the way we were outweighed the fear of any decisions I needed to make.*

I understood the betrayal and rejection my husband experienced. I understood the anger, fear, and pain. I have always understood, accepted, and validated his feelings, to the extent that I believed I felt them more than he did at times, if that's possible. Taking on his problems was not a conscious decision. I did it because I loved him.

Early on, I recognized the emptiness that seemed to fill his heart and soul. I wanted him to stop hurting. He seemed to have little joy or happiness inside. I wanted to fix that. Because I loved him and because I recognized his pain as familiar, I did everything I could to make him feel significant, loved, and wanted. In so doing, I lost a sense of myself and became codependent and addicted. Looking back, I recognize the complex web we wove around and through our relationship. A web created from our own holes as we searched and believed that we had found that one person and relationship that could make up for all the sense of loss we had experienced all our lives.

Our needs were never really articulated. They were simply perceived. So we never really knew if they could actually be met by the other. I think we were guided by our own unrecognized needs.

I had always experienced moments of being shut out by him. I would run after him consistently to bring him back to me. It served to reassure him that he was needed and loved and it alleviated my growing fear of being abandoned. It also kept me hooked. In running after him, I changed more and more about me so that I hardly recognized myself anymore. Yet all the while, I believed this was how it was supposed to be.

All my life, I had an inner sense of purpose, of destiny, of some reason for being alive. I never knew what it was. At times, I jumped from one idea to another as I continued to re-make and to redefine myself through my relationships. They came from within my own unfulfilled needs. None of these "makeovers" were conscious. It is only because I am now able to review and process from where I am now, that I am able to see clearly what happened and to understand that the road to dissolution was paved many, many years ago.

My inner sense of purpose did not always shine brightly. In fact, most often, I discounted those feelings as unrealistic and fantasy. It was relatively easy to discount them because of the powerful external messages received defining what a woman, wife, and mother ought to be and do. I believed them and did what I could to fulfill those expectations. I did it because of my own unhealed wounds of not belonging, of feeling abandoned, and unaccepted. Somehow, I perceived and then believed, that to be me was not appropriate or enough. Looking back, I thought that because these holes were created by perceived external events, that only external solutions could fill them. So I, like most of us, continued to look outside myself for the answers that would heal my wounds and for definition of this inner sense of purpose.

While our outer existence appeared to be happy and healthy, deep within both of us we longed for more. We didn't know that we were trying to swallow each other to keep from acknowledging that something was missing.

Many events, some smaller, some larger, occurred after two years of marriage that re-opened wounds. During the next thirteen years, I found myself reclaiming pieces, little by little, to keep the hurt from hurting too much. I did not recognize the fact that I was reclaiming pieces of myself. In hanging on to those pieces, I was beginning to outline what I was willing to accept for myself. Still, there was little reason to leave the relationship. I had not come to see my own relationship addiction.

When I added "career woman" to my many roles, suddenly flooding my inner being came a powerful, resounding knowingness that this was what had been missing in my life.

As I continued to teach and help people in pain, I knew that this work was not only what was missing in my life; it was what my life was meant to do.

I felt alive. I felt such joy from being able to help others. I began to recognize an insatiable hunger for more knowledge, more growth, and more of anything that would help me to help others. I could feel myself growing and learning from everyone whose path I crossed. In doing so, I needed him less and less to fill the holes in my heart. I began to heal and fill them myself. Yet there were many other hurts that came. Perhaps, because I was depending on him less and less, his fear of abandonment grew; and in his attempts to keep me, he did things that ended up hurting me, which resulted in my running away from him and towards my work. While he was supportive on one level, my growth and changing needs caused him much pain.

Who is to say what really happened? I believe we both, to this day, made right decisions and choices based on what we experienced at the time. We both chose to learn what we felt we needed to learn from those events. However disconnected they were - they were, and still are, our own lessons.

What I do know is that I redirected my focus and energy away from the relationship and toward myself. The affair was a catalyst for my own self-confrontation. *The emotional, psychological, physical, and spiritual pain outweighed the fear of confronting my own dependency and addiction.* I could make no decision about the relationship until I understood and accepted responsibility for my own feelings and needs.

I realized, in the past, that there were many times and events that I had created my own life choices around him. Avoiding my own dependency kept him reassured and prevented him from dealing with himself. Understanding this intellectually served to help me see how much of me I had invested and lost. It did not result in the absolute confrontation necessary to begin the healing and recovery from my own relationship addiction. The impact of that affair left me with nothing to lose.

As I became focused on my own recovery and growth, I reconnected with my own sense of spirituality. There was pain, but also a growing peace and knowledge that I was indeed enough for me. Still, I did not confront the issue of leaving the marriage. I simply chose to continue my own healing.

As I became focused on my own recovery and growth, I reconnected with my own sense of spirituality.

A year ago, there was a recognition and acceptance that I could never return to the marriage in the way it had existed. I did not want to dissolve the relationship. I had hoped that the marriage could be transformed. I knew that although I still loved him, I no longer needed to do the many things I had done before. Both ways of "need" were destructive to my sense of self and ultimately I believed they were destructive to him.

He experienced my healing self and desire to create a new relationship as an emotional rejection. Intellectually, I believe that he understood. But because of his own addiction and the years of living with "our habit," he ultimately was unable to accept this change. The last year leading to the break was full of anguish and chaos. The illusions and distortions, as well as the emerging truths flooded the relationship simultaneously.

Even as chaos surrounded me, I was at peace within. I knew with conviction that the "old way" was no longer healthy for me. I wished and hoped for a continuing relationship, but I didn't see it happening.

Chapter 17

During this time of healing, I was drawn to relationships with women. I acknowledged that I had denied my own emotional "feminine characteristics" for the masculine warrior traits that I believed were necessary to progress in this culture. The emotional bond was fully present and I began to recognize and to embrace the compassion, love, and respect we shared. I sensed a completion of my own circle of personal empowerment. We learned much from each other's pain, fear, strengths, and dreams. I learned also that being strong, direct, and aggressive did not mean that I could not be loving and compassionate. I learned to accept, to appreciate, and to express both my masculine and feminine selves. I learned that being loving, compassionate, and vulnerable did not mean weakness.

Looking back, I can understand his confusion and betrayal. I can accept his perception of conflicting messages. While I really did not wish to dissolve the marriage, the path I had chosen in my own recovery led me away from his presence as the center of my life. This perception of relationships I was involved with took on a "him versus woman" theme. By choosing this path, I accepted the responsibility and his blame for dissolving the marriage.

As with breaking any addiction, the last days are frightening, hurtful, and full of anger. While I never wished for the hurt and anguish, that was the way we parted. In my heart and soul, I have no regrets. My marriage brought many wonderful gifts for my own growth. His presence in my life allowed me

Spiritually, I am alive with both peace and joy. I am loved and taken care of. I feel the completeness and wholeness of the universe.

to become more intimate with myself and as a result, I was able to set myself free. In freeing myself, I know that he can also be free. This is how all of us were meant to be - free and whole. I am not floating on some illusionary cloud. I am aware that he may not choose to grasp the rightness of his freedom at this time. That is his right to make that choice. Whatever choices he will make will be right for him and will meet whatever needs he has. In dissolving this marriage, he is free to make those choices.

I am continuing the process of recovery. Intellectually, I have found the words that accurately describe the events and lessons of my relationships - the information has been enlightening and reaffirming.

Emotionally, the healing continues. Going within my holes - confronting them, accepting them, and forgiving myself for having them, brought me to a place of true love of self. I am able to laugh and to cry, to experience the breadth and the depth of emotions without conditions. I can truly feel again.

Spiritually, I am alive with both peace and joy. I am loved and taken care of. I feel the completeness and wholeness of the universe. I feel both the wonder and the comfort of the Creator. I feel the essence of God within and the knowingness that each of us has been blessed with special gifts that can serve the Highest vision of love and peace for all. In whatever manner we choose to manifest our gratitude and service to God as each of us chooses to perceive that, we can honor the gift of life and love within this manifestation then we can collectively heal ourselves and each other. Imagine a world of healing hearts!

Knowing that each of us has endured and survived the holes in our hearts brings us the knowledge that the strengths we mastered in surviving them can be channeled to affect transformation of self and therefore, the simultaneous healing of others. All things are very much possible.

Chapter 18

Truth, like trauma, is as you perceive it. This is a statement of inclusivity. This philosophy eliminates wrongness and blame. Truth is what is real at whatever place in time you are in your personal evolution. Your personal truth meets the physical, emotional, intellectual, and spiritual needs that exist at that moment. Truth like personal growth is transitory, ever shifting, ever changing. It is the belief in the fixed absoluteness of truth, the exclusivity of it that brings difficulty, conflict, blame, and wrongness.

When I was three, I saw the world through the eyes of three. Whatever interpretation I created based on my experience is not fantasy, but real and true. Real and true enough to result in deep emotional experiences that served to imprint my life and to further my own growth and journey.

When I was 23, those events of 3 were still real and true. What was different was the way in which I perceived them given 20 additional years of experience. My perception of those events, as well as the events of the present, are also real and true. Neither is more right nor more wrong.

Personal growth is the continual integration of all levels of truth without discounting or disowning them. This integration and acceptance leads to the acceptance of the self, and therefore to the acceptance of others.

Unfortunately, everyone does not grow or evolve at the same pace. Conflict arises when people are at two different levels of truth. Both perceptions are true, both are right, yet both cannot accept the differences in

Understanding and accepting my own perception of truth is what has allowed me the acceptance and marriage of my masculine and feminine self.

perceptions. It is the exclusive, all-or-nothing, only one right way that leads us to the desire and battle to change either the self or another self. This is the fixed absoluteness that creates the foundation for blame and wrongness. Relationships like these are competitive. There is always a winner and a loser. Since we are conditioned to devalue the loser, we find ourselves doing whatever is necessary to prevent being the loser. Because truth is as it is perceived, accepting one's own truth becomes accepting another's perception. There is no competition or devaluing of another. There is acceptance and a deeper understanding that each of us perceives what we need to at different times in our lives.

When we stop making ourselves wrong, we stop making others right. When we stop blaming ourselves, we stop blaming others. When we accept our own truths, we open to the truths of others. In this way, we draw to ourselves the light and joy of all experiences and our own growth becomes less painful. We begin the healing of ourselves and therefore allow the healing of others.

Accepting the truth of the moment is what enables us to accept the rules or external messages at certain times in our lives. It is also what enables us to question and to leave them at other times in our lives. Because our truth is based on our own needs within a given circumstance or time period, we enter into relationships, careers or experiences freely and fully. When the needs change, as all things must of necessity do, the needs may no longer be met within the same framework of that initial truth. Instead of denouncing or rejecting it, accepting that those relationships, careers or experiences have fully met the initial needs allows the freedom to continue one's own journey without conflict, fear or wrongness. In a sense, it is much like a completion of classroom requirements.

Understanding and accepting my own perception of truth is what has allowed me to move on, to continue my own journey. It is what has allowed me to disengage from any battles with those I choose to leave. It is the reason for my non-attachment and acceptance of the dissolution of my marriage, of the completion of my work within the "system," of the resolution of my parent-child relationship, of the integration of my cultural identity, and the acceptance and marriage of my masculine and feminine self. It is the foundation for my sense of spiritual wholeness.

It enables me to seek the highest meaning of all experiences with a knowingness that truth brings me peace, serenity, joy, and happiness. Truth is the filling of my soul and the filling of all beings. It is our sense of completion and wholeness.

Like trauma, truth is as we perceive it. Understanding and accepting our holes in our hearts without fear of wrongness or loss is the healing and the sense of wholeness we seek all our lives. For even the creation of those holes brings a deeper understanding of life and personal purpose.

The acceptance of emotions deeply felt from within those holes teaches us compassion and empathy for ourselves and for others. The acceptance of our survival skills brings the determination to confront obstacles or challenges and motivates our forward movement on life's journey. Together, this acceptance is the healing of our holes; it is the freeing of one's spirit and the joy of the completion of our wholeness.

When we value all aspects of our lives, we value all aspects of ourselves. When we allow for the rightness of all people, places, and things as right for that moment and place in time, we allow for rightness of self. When we allow our own truth, we allow the truth of others. In this way, we are indeed free in mind, body, and soul.

Chapter 19

My personal journey continues. There is a newness about it however. I have experienced a rebirth and a return to self simultaneously. I am now choosing to grow with joy after a lifetime of experiencing growth through pain. In this way, I am free ... truly free at last!

My personal journey continues as life itself continues. I recognize that as long as I live I shall always continue to question, to seek the highest truth and understanding of myself in the moment. This story is my understanding of the holes in my heart as it exists today. If I had to choose one word to accurately describe the lesson so far, it would be "inclusivity. "

I am not advocating the dissolution of relationships: marital, parent-child, or friendships. I am not advocating any particular philosophy or lifestyle. I am not advocating for any person, place or thing that eludes to the "one way," the "one truth," the "only thing," that will bring about "true" healing, compassion, love or success. It is the "one" anything that exemplifies the dualism, the externalization that exists in our culture. It is not fitting into this "one" anything that caused the hole in my heart. There is no one way. There is simply your way.

The purity of mind, heart, and soul of the infant symbolize the essence and spirit of love, life, truth, and freedom. The infant knows nothing of any specific appropriate way to be. Being held, being loved, being free to cry, to laugh, to feel, and to experience comes from within that infant. There are no barriers or obstacles, no holes that exist within the infant. Loving is unconditional, laughter and pain are full without restraint. Pleasure and joy are

The personal journey through life is just that - personal. We arrive at whatever place we choose as we need to.

expressed with the wholeness of the being. It is external messages that restrict, contain, and inhibit the fullness and openness of that infant. It is external judgment that becomes internalized; and in a very short time, the infant learns conditional living. The spirit of that infant remembers the fullness of its beginning. Regardless of the experiences along the way, there is always the knowingness that there was a time when living was living, and not merely surviving or existing.

No person, place or thing has a monopoly on the answers to life. Each of us is unique and special with our own way of perceiving our own life needs and desires. I believe that when we condemn or belittle others for their own personal choices, we create an exclusivity that results in fear, anger, wrongness, and blame. It not only hurts others, but more importantly, we restrict and confine our own spirit.

I believe that is why any movement for social transformation that begins outside ourselves creates further entrenchment of rules, roles, and conflict. No one person, group or thought can possess the one answer to emotional healing or intellectual growth. No one owns God. No one person, group or thought is more evolved or better than another. The personal journey through life is just that - personal. We arrive at whatever place we choose as we need to. We make whatever decisions and choices necessary at that time. Our desire to change or not, is a personal decision that I made whenever the time is right for that decision. People, places, and things are present in our life as we need them. They can teach us much about ourselves, if we choose to learn. If we choose not to learn it, it's simply because we choose not to learn. That is neither right nor wrong.

The many rules, roles, and messages in our life provide us with a variety of knowledge and guidelines that we can accept or reject as we need to. Therefore, there is only a continuing path of self discovery, self awareness, of self-acceptance and self-love.

As I continue my journey, I am more fully aware of the wonder and miracles of human beings. I appreciate all the information available to us for our own choices. I am grateful for the variety of ways I can pursue the healing of my own emotional pain. I feel such comfort in the many ways that God is perceived. I rejoice in the many ways male and female roles are experienced. Whether or not I subscribe to any particular belief or lifestyle is not the issue. What is important to me is that all ways are valid and are truth as interpreted by the individual. It is the availability of choices that is freeing.

I recognize that many will continue to place judgment and to condemn others for choices. I have experienced those condemnations and judgments. Regardless of where those judgments come from, it is the right of others to have them. Regardless of how loudly they may protest, I look within myself and know that I am living my own life, by whatever is right for me at this time. I do not feel the need to defend the position because I no longer need permission to be.

In not seeking permission, I am not seeking approval or acceptance for my existence. Therefore, I have given away the fear that there is not enough love, not enough spirituality, or not enough persons who will be able to make me feel complete and whole. I recognize all of the elements of myself — as uniquely mine. I experience the world through my own vision. I feel love, trust, peace, and joy freely. From within me I am able to give and receive it from others freely because I no longer need it to fill the holes in my heart.

THREE

CHOOSING TO GROW

Chapter 20

Sitting here at the dining room table, I marvel at the depth of understanding I have gained about myself and others through writing this story. That is so much the way of personal growth. Even as we arrive at one level of understanding, we recognize that while we know more, we know less. My life continues to be a series of events that allow for more self-discovery. It is not that life has suddenly more to offer; it is that I am offering more to life. I am offering an openness to all possibilities and all realities. I am continuing to acknowledge many more "truths" about myself and how those "truths" affected me and in some cases, continue to affect me.

Like Dorothy in the *Wizard of Oz*, I have been travelling that yellow brick road on a journey that led me home where I began. I have crossed paths with many people on my way. Each person has given me the gift of knowledge, of compassion, of courage, and inspiration. Each lesson brought as many questions as it did answers. The process has allowed my journey to continue.

It isn't that my life has been remarkable by external measures. It hasn't been marked with tremendous obstacles or overwhelming contributions. However, it is the very "ordinary-ness" of life that is in itself remarkable. It is the gifts received from so many. It is the choices I made which led me to a greater understanding of myself and therefore of others. It is the way in which I have chosen to perceive my life and myself that brings me a sense of empowerment and serenity of soul. Through my quest for knowledge and my choice to look within, I have been able to heal the holes in my heart. In healing the holes in my heart, I have returned home, freeing my spirit from conditional living and loving.

On my journey, I have had to confront many external messages about who, what, how, and why I am. Rather than to reject these messages, I fully grasped them, experienced them, and learned from them. As I continue to grow, I left many of them behind. My learning has been inspired by the many people I have known in my life. Broken, battered, bruised, and tormented spirits; they represented each of us. Their weaknesses are reflections of our own fears, hurts, and anger. Their strengths tell us of the incredible power and will of the spirit.

I found in their faces and hearts, the same need to be free of the cages we lock ourselves in because we are unable to fully live within the superficial external rules and conditions placed upon us. They are not simply "they." They are "we."

Conditional living and loving restrictions confine our spirits. It is the most unnatural way to live life to its fullest. Each of us ordinary people knows the feeling of not belonging or the fear of not being enough or the pain of being judged or the fear of loss. Each of us knows the frustration of being misunderstood. We have all heard the messages of winners and losers, of better than and less than, of rightness and wrongness.

From the basic definition of masculinity and femininity to the absoluteness of spirituality, these dualistic, externalized messages touch and trap us all. For as truly spiritual and physical beings, we cannot fully live within all of the confines of every externalized condition of living. We cannot fully trust or depend upon external sources for our own inner sense of "validation, acceptance, and approval." The truth in that statement is in our own pain, fear, and anger. If we are only able to feel loved, needed, and secure because we receive it from outside ourselves, then we are destined to feel unloved, unneeded, and insecure when it is withdrawn. The fear of losing it or the actual loss of it creates a greater need to hang onto it. We increase our fear that there will not be enough for us all.

Each person along the way may not have always appeared to be broken and battered. Yet, deep within them there was a knowingness that they had much in common with one another. Because we live within the same external conditions, there can be no escape from the impact these messages will have or have had on our lives. We all experience the holes in our hearts as we fail to fit neatly into all of the definitions of who and what we should be.

All of our lives we have heard these messages. Most of us, have accepted a greater portion of these messages to the extent that we have created truths from them. Because truth is as we perceive it, there is no wrongness that comes with our belief in them. The wrongness comes when we are unable to live those truths absolutely. The judgment of wrongness comes from others who may be able to absolutely live and fit within that particular truth.

For example, we have all heard and felt the separateness of being male and of being female. We can readily recite masculine characteristics and differentiate them from feminine characteristics. We learned that to be aggressive, goal-oriented, strong, and powerful is appropriate for men. Being feminine is defined as quieter, passive, nurturing, emotional, and intuitive. What happens when the spirit lives within a physical body that is logical and goal-oriented; and within an emotional body that is sensitive and compassionate? Is that person masculine or feminine by definition? Often she is labelled, criticized or otherwise ostracized for her very existence. Conversely, if a spirit dwells within a physical form that is male; within an emotional body that is sensitive, nurturing, and compassionate and within an intellectual body that relies on intuition rather than logic, is that being accepted wholly as masculine? Often he is chastised for his lack of masculinity.

We are more than gender dictates physically and sexually. We are more than color defines. We are more than religion validates. We are more than our intellect rationalizes.

I have learned from the men whose paths I've crossed how to be strong, courageous, and bold. I've learned to fight my battles as a warrior, with an analytical mind, with perseverance, and loyalty to the mission. I have also learned how painful it is to repress feelings of fear, of pain, and of powerlessness. I have felt their pain of being misunderstood and their fear of being rejected. I recognized their confusion and frustration of not always fitting the image of what they were told they should be.

I have seen and experienced the build-up of these internalized fears and hurts as they explode, sometimes violently, upon the very persons they love and need. I have felt the pain of their addiction to that one person or relationship that makes it easier to be a male. I acknowledged and accepted those lessons because I found much of myself in those men. I recognized those same fears and hurts as my own. I reaffirmed my own strengths and warrior spirit as I related to theirs. I gained both their approval and respect for my masculine traits, yet I also experienced rejection of my female form. The spirit of these men, then as now, are trapped by externalized definitions of being male. In being masculine, there is a denial or devaluing of what is defined as feminine. The denial, minimization or devaluing of emotion is intensely painful because it necessitates the denial of a whole part of one's self. Yet, being male, being masculine, is still understood and accepted as being powerful and right. Many men are striving to fit neatly within that definition and finding it increasingly difficult to be free.

Women who experience these masculine characteristics within them, suffer greatly both personally and within their relationships to other women. Identifying and accepting the masculine part of me often necessitated my denial of my femininity and my connection to my feminine world. As I was growing up, there were few female role models who embodied the masculine warrior spirit while retaining the "appropriate" female traits as defined by external "truths." The women I admired were strong, aggressive, and goal-oriented. These women were often denounced and criticized for their lack of "appropriateness." Often they were characterized as domineering, arrogant, cold-hearted, man-hating women. These degrading and demoralizing statements were so prevalent that many of these women were not only attacked by the male world, they were excluded from the female world. What message was learned from these painful attacks by those of us who identified with these female warriors?

Women were, and still are, faced with an "either-or" decision-making. Belonging, approval, and acceptance are conditional for both men and women. Those conditions are based upon what has been defined as appropriate by external messages.

Many women who believed it appropriate to be passive, submissive, nurturing, and dependent believe so out of a greater need to belong to sanctioned rules of being female. This truth often allows for the external victimization of the physical, emotional, and intellectual body. I have learned from the culture's victims how to be dependent, to be submissive, and to be responsible for any relationship. I have felt the pain of physical weakness and the betrayal of emotions. I have seen the reflection of the powerlessness of being female as it bursts the dam of confusion and frustration. I have seen and felt the depth of despair and the heights of hope from behind the bruised faces, from within the broken hearts, and battered souls. I have learned how to survive the oppression of the spirit from these incredible women. Yet, from these same women, I have experienced compassion, unconditional love, and acceptance

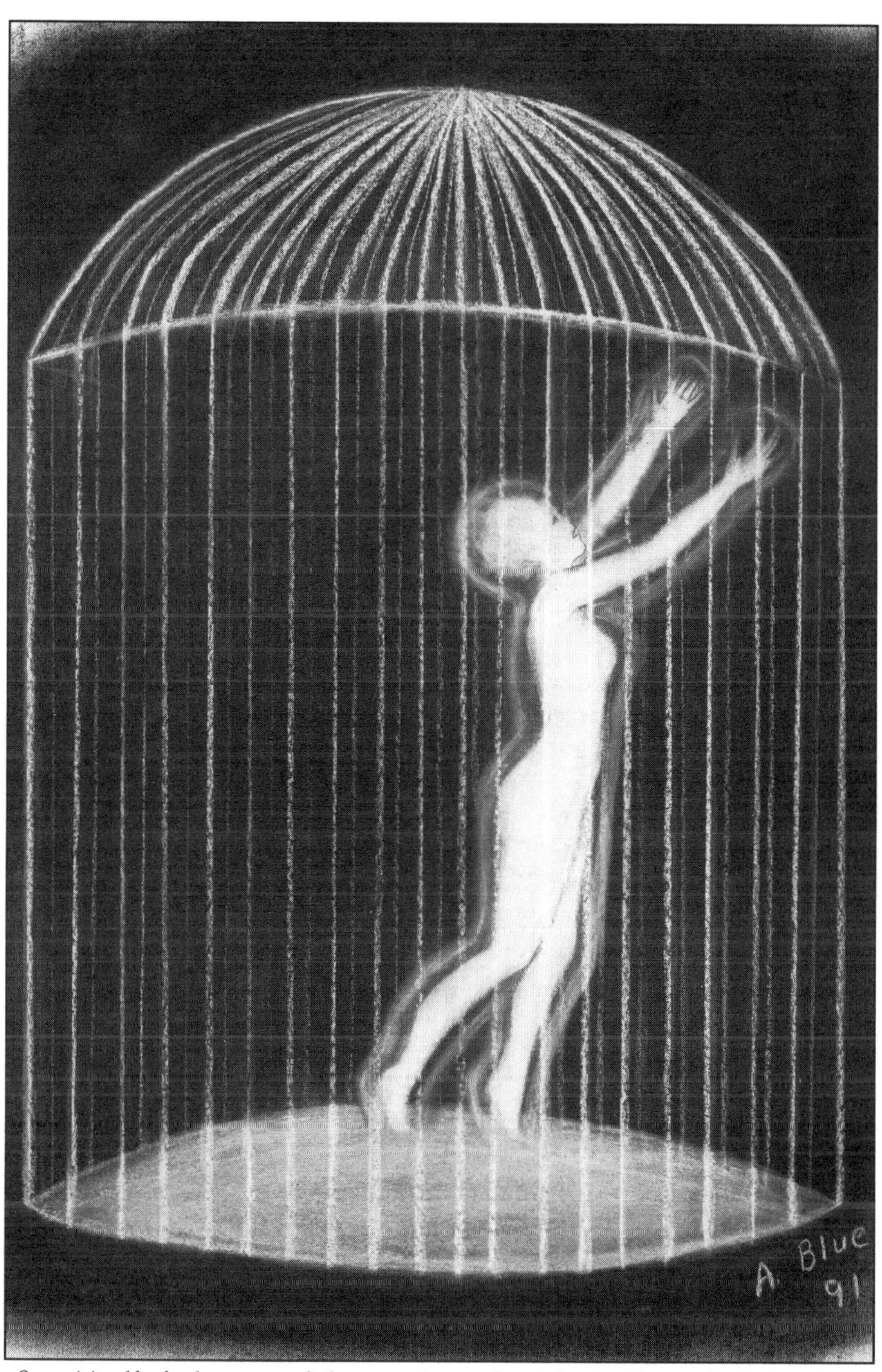

Our spiritual body, the essence of who we are, is caged and chastised for its unbridled energy, for its limitless possibilities, for its unconditional living.

in much the same way that I have experienced it from men whose spirits were also oppressed.

Like Dorothy, my greatest understanding of myself did not come from those we perceive to be in power. My greatest and most valued gifts came from those whose physical, intellectual, and emotional selves were outcast and judged.

It was from these magical people that I found that we are all hurting from our own holes in our hearts. I learned that there is no one who can neatly fit into all of the categories we learned we should belong to. I learned that no one is better which means that no one is less than. There is no rightness and wrongness. No one way, one truth, one place, one person or one thing that is absolute truth. How we perceive our lives, our selves, our Creator or our reason to be can only be defined by the self.

I learned that we all have many holes in our hearts that come from many different experiences. Each experience resulted in feelings of loss ... loss of love, loss of security, loss of belonging or loss of freedom. We spend a lifetime trying to overcome our loss so that we can heal those wounds. So, whose rules are they? Where do they come from? Why do we strive so hard to fit into rules that bring us such pain, fear, and anger?

Healing the wounds comes from within, for it is from within that we are wounded. We have coerced our outer selves, physical, emotional, and intellectual bodies to conform to rules that are not always valid. Our spiritual body, the essence of who we are, is caged and chastised for its unbridled energy, for its limitless possibilities, for its unconditional living. Our search for home is the return to that inner knowingness that we are enough, that there is enough.

Chapter 21

From our healing hearts we can recognize that these rules we strive so hard to belong to were also created from within the holes in our hearts.

Just as Dorothy created her disillusionment with her physical existence, so did she create the disillusionment of her fantasy. When she perceived that her environment was unresponsive to her needs, she held a fantasy environment responsible to fill her needs. Yet, because the hole existed within her own heart; she had to learn to rely upon herself to find her way home. Her journey was not unlike our own journeys. Like her, we look to others for answers, for direction, for strength, courage, and compassion. Like her, we meet many who mirror the very answer within us that we need to further our own journeys. Like her, our own unconquerable spirits will press us onward, relentlessly in pursuit of its freedom because that is what we are all meant to be - free.

As Dorothy came to accept her creation of disillusionment, she came to realize the power of her own creation. As she confronted each dimension of her fears, she found that when *the pain from the thought of not returning home outweighed fear,* she was able to let go and to take the risk of continuing her journey. Dorothy learned to rely upon her intuition, compassion, logic, and strength to return home. Like her, it was the integrating of both masculine and feminine characteristics that frees our spirit. She also found that as her self-acceptance grew, so did her acceptance of others. By her example, she allowed others to find the confidence, love, compassion, and courage within themselves. The inclusivity of all her experiences mirrored the many dimensions of her own self. Her journey was simply the conscious awareness of the meaning of those experiences.

Through and by her own creation, fantasy and reality were intertwined, both holding real truths and levels of understanding. What began as real disillusionment became real freedom upon her return home. There is indeed, *no place like home.*

Throughout my life, I have often been thanked for the many gifts I have given to others. Yet, somehow, it is I that has been blessed by their gifts of self. The pain I witnessed from men trapped by their own creation of reality, of masculinity incomplete, of needs unfulfilled, and of faraway fantasies, was not unlike my own pain. The fears I accepted from women overwhelmed by their sense of powerlessness and their creation of fantasy to comfort and to deny their own needs was the mirror of my own fears. Listening, acknowledging, and accepting the mirror images of my own wounds allowed me to accept my own pain and fear; and therefore allowed me to accept theirs.

Their courage and determination to meet each obstacle inspired me to renew my own commitment to self. I learned so much about the will of our own spirit. I felt deeply the persistence of our own right to be.

I believe we saw in each other the unconditional love and acceptance of empowered beings. They taught me to look beyond the anger and violence, beyond the weakness of the physical body, beyond the emotional confusion, beyond the rigid, inflexible stereotypes of all of us into the depths of their souls. I learned these things as I experienced their anger and violence, their physical pain, their emotional confusion, and the same rigid, inflexible stereotypes inflicted upon me. It is not that I was able to connect with each of these people - sometimes it was the disconnection that brought me to these discoveries. It was these people as they were, not as they had become that inspired me. It was the commonality of the holes in our hearts that allowed me to heal my own wounds. It is because of the commonality of our wounds that I was inspired to write this story.

What is remarkable about being ordinary is the commonality, the inter-connectedness, the interdependency, and oneness of us all. It is the knowledge that our inner spirits are meant to be free from the limitations of our outer selves. In our freedom, we do not limit our love and compassion for ourselves or for others. In our freedom we place no restrictions on what we must and should be.

It is not unlike the awareness that happens when lying on a grassy hill looking up at the billowing clouds. If one continues to contemplate clouds; hows, wheres, and whys begin to formulate in one's mind.

We can choose to accept truth as it serves to further our own paths and we can let it go when its purpose has been served. In our "ordinary-ness" there is the greatness of our spirit as perfect beings just as we were created. There is the knowledge that each of us has a special purpose and has been blessed with special gifts designed to enhance our existence.

We were created from the purity of unconditional love by our Creator. That love was not meant to be devalued or degraded, confined or restricted. That love was not meant to be used in judgment of another. That love was meant to bring us life and the gift of ourselves to one another. It was meant to fill us with abundance. I am realizing that the very gifts I am thanked for, are the same gifts I have received.

These special people taught me much about myself. Regardless of the positive or negative interaction within the relationships, the lessons have had a positive impact on my personal growth. I chose to learn these lessons, sometimes painfully, sometimes joyfully; but always with a commitment to understanding and knowing more about myself.

It is in the choosing that the gift of self-discovery, self-acceptance, and self-love lie waiting. In choosing to feel the anger, fear or hurt, one chooses one level of understanding. In choosing to look beyond anger, fear and hurt, one chooses yet another level of understanding and so on. Because each of us, as free independent beings, sees truth as it is relevant to us, we come to understand and to know all levels of truth as it applies to our self and to the selves of others.

As the process of growth continues, there is often a feeling of confusion and conflict as one leaves one level of truth and enters another. As one layer of anger, fear or hurt is peeled away by understanding, there is another layer to replace it. With the understanding comes an increased feeling of peace, serenity, and an increased awareness and acuity of vision.

It is not unlike the awareness that happens when lying on a grassy hill looking up at the billowing clouds. At first glance, the awareness of those clouds is that they are simply there. If one continues to contemplate clouds; hows, wheres, and whys begin to formulate in one's mind. Perhaps, they even begin to take on shapes.

The emotions experienced during this process may range from com-placency to confusion or frustration to joy. The outer manifestation of clouds has not changed. Our inner questioning has changed our perception and therefore the meaning these clouds hold for us at that one moment in time. This is true of anger, fear, hurt, joy and peace as well as many other emotions.

It is in choosing growth that we free our spirits. It is in choosing to grow that we arrive where we began - connected to one another and to all things. It is in choosing to grow that we leave levels of self-blame, guilt, wrongness, anger, and fear, as well as blaming others. We leave judgment, approval or disapproval. We leave conditional living. We leave each level of growth with the inner knowingness that every truth has served a special purpose. In understanding that purpose, we free ourselves from negative thinking or ways of being. We free ourselves from setting limits and barriers for ourselves and therefore, we free others from the same restrictions and confinements of the spirit. When we arrive at each new level of understanding, there is a sense of returning home. The process continues indefinitely. It is simply a matter of choosing.

Epilogue

This story is not meant to minimize or discount real pain, sorrow, and anger. This story is not meant to be a bandaid for the real suffering of our Earth's people. Rather, the purpose is to validate that same suffering without judgment of whose pain is greater. Each of us experiences trauma as real, relevant, and true for us. Each of us experiences truth, peace, and serenity as just as real and relevant. By giving our experiences permission to be felt and understood fully, we remove limitations and restrictions on living. We give permission to ourselves by simply choosing to do so. By the same token, if we choose to perceive our selves as victims, we must acknowledge that our perceptions of others is through the eyes of a victim. If we choose to perceive ourselves as "right," we must acknowledge that we perceive others from a place of "rightness" and if they are not just as we are, then we will always see them as "wrong." If we perceive life as threatening, then we will approach all things and people from a place of fear.

Whatever our expectations are, they are so manifested. Whatever our fears are, we will find fear waiting for us. If we perceive our selves as having value, worth, and significance, we will find it in others. It is all in the way we choose to perceive it.

I ran away many times in my life from real pain, confusion, and anger. Trauma was only as I perceived it. When I stopped running, I discovered that I was not running away from those events, I was running away from myself. I discovered many truths in my search for inner peace. Truth was and is as I perceive it. Both the trauma and the truth brought me full circle to where I began.

My life is "ordinary." How I have chosen to view the lessons in my life is what brings me the knowingness that all life is "extra-ordinary."

I have arrived at the Emerald City with all of the joy, hope, and elation experienced by my friends in the Land of Oz. Like them, I know that many

There is no need to cling to the joy and the peace of that Emerald City out of fear of losing it. I know that I can return here anytime I choose to because the Emerald City exists within me.

more lessons lie ahead. Yet, rather than fearing what is unknown, I welcome them as additional stepping stones on my journey. There is no need to cling to the joy and peace of that Emerald City out of fear of losing it. I know that I can return here anytime I choose to because the Emerald City exists within me.

For now, I choose to experience life fully and unconditionally with the knowledge that all things are possible.

Healing the holes in our hearts happens when we choose to acknowledge that they exist, when we choose to understand where they come from, and when we choose to learn from them. In so doing, we can let go of anger, blame, fear, and wrongness. In letting go, we return to the freedom of our spirit as we all were when life began. In freeing our spirit, all things are indeed possible. Freeing the spirit is both empowering and powerful.

Returning home is the return to the abundance of love, trust in the self, and limitless faith. It is the knowledge that we were each given a special gift of our own existence. Through our appreciation of ourselves, we appreciate others; for we are all, inclusively, part of the whole human race.

Indeed, there is no place like home, for home is where we celebrate life....

About the Author

I was born of Japanese, African-American, Native-American, and Caucasian-American descent.   Being a female or multicultural is not significant in and of itself. Being born in the middle of a color and cultural continuum in our society was difficult and wounding to my sense of cultural identity. Being born female in our society was wounding to my sexual identity. Being born to two loving people who brought with them all of their own wounds and unhealed scars of this dysfunctional society was wounding to my inner spiritual identity. Alcoholism, abuse, and racism touched me in ways that left me searching all my life for the one person, the one accomplishment, the one solution that would fill the hole in my heart. I grew up in a rigid military family system within a rigid military environment. I married into that same dysfunctional system - not because I loved it, but because it was familiar. I was comfortable with being uncomfortable. My work with substance abuse, family violence, and cultural issues was a way to fix what was broken in our society. But it was more than that. It was my subconscious way of fixing the wounds in my soul. Throughout my marriage, my parenting, and my professional life, I have been giving to get. The ability to relate to the military, to alcoholics and drug addicts, to battered women and children, to the racially oppressed were gifts of my wounds. Still, no matter what I had accomplished, I was left with a deep sense of inadequacy. The day I became painfully aware that I was passing my wounds to my daughter - marked the beginning of my own discovery and recovery.

My whole life has changed. Though divorced, I share an enriched, whole relationship with my former spouse. Though separated from the military, I have a deeper compassion for the people within that system. Though away from my direct counseling with family violence, substance abuse, and cultural issues, I can now bring a wholeness, a deeper understanding, and a magic of care and concern to effectively help in whatever ways I can.

The journey is really all about being - being free to be.

From the instant of my birth, my journey has been filled with lessons learned from everyone whose path I've crossed. It has been learning these lessons that broadens my journey. If you would like to share your thoughts, feelings or experiences with me, you may reach me by writing to this address:

Elaine M. Whitefeather
P.O. Box 292
Fair Oaks, CA 95628

For additional copies of <u>Healing the Holes in My Heart</u> or for copies of <u>The Nuffs, Not So Sure, and the Wanna Be's</u>, please write to:

Elaine M. Whitefeather
P.O. Box 292
Fair Oaks, CA 95628

Elaine Bready is also available for lectures, workshops, and to appear as a guest speaker in your area. Please contact us at the above address for further information.

A. Blue
'91